BE~~~~

——OF THE——

WORLD

BEARS

—— OF THE ——

WORLD

Paul Ward & Suzanne Kynaston

BLANDFORD

A BLANDFORD BOOK

This paperback edition first published in the UK 1999 by Blandford
A Cassell imprint

Cassell plc,
Wellington House
125 Strand
London WC2R 0BB

www.cassell.co.uk

Hardback edition published in the UK by Blandford 1995

Distributed in the United States by Sterling Publishing Co., Inc.,
387 Park Avenue South, New York, NY 10016-8810

A Cataloguing-in-Publication Data entry for this title is available and may be
obtained from the British Library

ISBN 0-7137-2787-X

Typeset by Keystroke, Wolverhampton, UK

Printed in Hong Kong by Colourcraft Ltd

Contents

Acknowledgements

It is not possible to write a book of this type without the help of a number of other people; in this particular case we have drawn heavily on the work of many scientists researching various aspects of bear natural history. We have given a list of key books and papers in the further reading at the end; here we would like to acknowledge the other people whose work has been of use to us. Much of the known information on polar bears comes from the long-term research of I. Stirling, M. Ramsay, A. Derocher and C. Pond. The giant panda has been most thoroughly covered by G. Schaller (and Chinese co-workers), D. Reid and D. Morris. American bears have been studied by S. Herrero, M. Pelton, D. Garshelis, E. Hellgren, R. Nelson, J. and F. Craighead, G. and M. Folk and J. Hunt. Other people to whom we are indebted are C. Servheen, J. A. Mills, A. Ames, G. Law, S. O'Brien, F. L. Bunnell, T. Hamilton, R. C. Best, D. Weinhardt, B. Peyton, K. Johnson, J. McKinnon, J. Seidenstecker, B. Kurten, M. Anderson, B. Sanders and M. Gimbutas.

In addition we would also like to thank Stuart Booth, our long-suffering editor; Peter and Gillian Mill; David and Pamela Maitland; and also our families for their advice, encouragement and assistance; and, finally, the staff of the Edward Boyle Library (University of Leeds) for their help in securing books and papers.

S.K. & P.W.

Illustration Credits

Preface

In this book we have tried to portray bears as more than just an interesting group of animals. Although many aspects of their biology are fascinating, our personal feeling is that bears are also symbolic of the natural world, both in their own right and in the way that we, as human beings, treat them.

We are both mammal biologists and so, of all animals, mammals are the group with which we are the most familiar and with which we have had the most dealings. It has to be said that scientists frequently have a very different view of animals than do other people; in our experience this is often a very sterile attitude in which the animals are merely the objects of scrutiny and experiment. Although this is not a universal phenomenon among the scientific community, we have encountered it too often; at conferences we listen to the results of spectacular research being delivered with no enthusiasm or excitement. We feel that this is somehow demeaning, both to the animal and to the scientist. For neither of us has any animal become so familiar a sight that we fail to feel a sense of excitement at it. Both of us recognize that we have experienced some of our best moments sharing the lives of animals. In this book we wanted to convey this.

What we have tried to do is present a picture which encompasses science, natural history and that other deeper, almost spiritual, aspect of bears. We hope that we have managed to do this and that, as you read this book, you too will become engrossed in the stories of their lives and deaths.

We start by explaining how and why bears have meant so much to Man from early in our evolutionary history, how they have bridged the gap between the natural and spiritual worlds and how, even today, they hold a special place in our society. We then go on to describe the bears' position and uniqueness among carnivores and to introduce the living species. The evolutionary history of bears, how they live, what they eat and how they cope with their habitats is followed by a look at their behaviour. Finally, we return to the inter-relationship they have with Man, how they suffer by our hand and how attempts are being made to reverse the damage that we have done.

We realize that, since you are reading this, we are probably preaching to the already converted; maybe for some of you this will not be the case but for others maybe we can introduce new thoughts. Whatever the case, the provision of new facts was only part of the reason for this book being written; putting bears under the spotlight of sympathetic and caring scrutiny was the principal aim. We hope you enjoy the story.

S.K. & P.W.
Leeds
England

Chapter 1

Spirits of the Wilderness

For many people, bears symbolize either strength and power, or warmth and security; images which are strongly linked to the portrayal of these animals in advertisements, cartoons, movies and as popular toys. For an animal to be equally associated with such strongly conflicting emotions in human beings is rare and emphasizes the cultural impact which bears possess for many different peoples. This popularity is not merely a modern phenomenon, but has been found across the northern hemisphere since Paleolithic times wherever bears and human beings have co-existed.

BEARS AND EARLY MAN

The earliest relationship between Man and bears is thought to have involved Neanderthals (an early race of *Homo sapiens*) and the now extinct European cave bear, when the two both occupied areas of Europe during the last interglacial and earlier part of the last glaciation some 200,000–75,000 years ago.

Possible evidence of such cave-bear worship was discovered by Emil Bächler, between 1917 and 1922, in the Drachenloch Cave, situated in the Swiss Alps. Remains from here have been dated to the last interglacial; among them was a large stone chest containing several cave-bear skulls, all of which were pointing towards the entrance of the cave. Some of these skulls had small stones arranged around them while others were set on stone slabs; in one case, a skull had bear thigh bones pushed through the eye-sockets and, in another, similar bones had been inserted beneath the snout. However, there have been a number of discrepancies regarding the details of such finds and there is very little other evidence of Man's presence in the cave (such as flint implements and burnt bones), causing some scientists to doubt the explanation of the discovery, instead regarding the phenomena as the result of natural causes.

Konrad Hormann, excavating Petershöhle Cave in southern Germany between 1916 and 1922, found closet-like niches in the walls, each containing five cave-bear skulls surrounded by rocks. This also suggests some form of cave-bear worship, although again it has been argued that this arrangement may have come about through natural processes.

Firmer evidence of ritual behaviour by Neanderthal Man comes in the form of a rectangular pit covered with a heavy stone slab, found in the Régourdu Cave in southern France. Originally described by the French prehistorian, Eugène Bonifay, in the 1960s, the pit is believed to be a Neanderthal grave into which various 'offerings' have been made, including several bones from brown bears (*Ursus arctos*); the positioning of these bones does suggest intentional placement.

Cro-Magnon (Modern) Man first appeared in Europe about 35,000 years ago; from this time evidence of bear-worship becomes more obvious as the incidence of paintings, sculptures and engravings increases. Some doubt still remains, however, as to whether the species represented is the cave bear (*Ursus spelaeus*) or the European brown bear (*U. arctos arctos*).

The earliest Paleolithic art, found associated with the remains of Ancient peoples, dates from about 30,000 years ago. There are some 100 representations of bears recorded and most are believed to depict the brown bear.

Some unusual bear-engravings, such as one found in Trois-Frères Cave at Ariège, France, appear to show the animal pierced by spears and, in this particular case, vomiting blood. Such cave-paintings are usually interpreted as works of sympathetic magic where, by drawing an animal, especially with a spear in it, a hunter gained influence over the real animal and ensured a successful hunt. However, bear-rites and ceremonies may also be depicted; in a cave at Pechialet in the Dordogne, France, is a pictograph which has been interpreted as two men dancing with a bear.

It has been noted that bears are always represented singly in such cave-paintings, whereas most other animals appear in pairs. It is believed that this may possibly be due to the bear's embodiment of both female and male characteristics: maternal care and paternal ferocity.

Norbert Casteret, on excavating a cave near Montespan, France, unearthed a headless clay sculpture of what is believed to be a bear lying on its belly. It was a life-size model measuring about 1m (39in) in length and 0.5m (19in) in height. Evidence points to the fact that the head had been deliberately removed and it is thought that the presence of a central hole in the truncated neck allowed the insertion of a stick upon which a bear's skull was placed. The sculpture was covered with spear marks and the skull of a young bear was found between the forepaws, suggesting that the figure may have been used as part of a hunting ritual.

Bears have been represented in paintings and sculptures since Man first started to express images 30,000 years ago. Here, a bear head is represented on a Neolithic stone club from Finland dating from the second millenium BC.

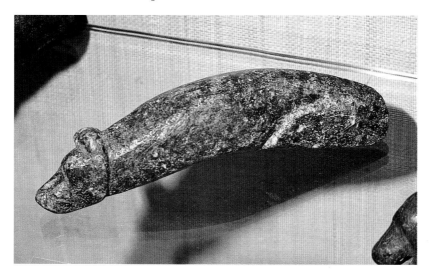

THE BEAR AS AN OBJECT OF WORSHIP

Bears have assumed the status of sacred animal to a considerable number of different peoples; a fact which begs the question as to why they are so popular as objects of worship.

Bears can be very dangerous animals; people may easily be mauled should they come across them unawares. Consequently, they have been both greatly feared and also held in considerable respect throughout the ages. Numerous North American Indian tribes have practised various rites aimed at preventing themselves from being attacked. Hunters of some northern Athapaskan tribes, for example, poked out the eyes and cut off the forepaws of the bear after they had killed it; this, they believed, prevented the animal from seeing its killers and its spirit from hunting them.

However, and more importantly, a kind of kinship seems to have existed between indigenous peoples and bears, brought about by similarities which early human beings saw between themselves and the animal, characteristics which did not exist in any other beast. Bears walk like human beings, placing both heel and toe on the ground, leaving a heel-, arch- and-toe foot-print uncannily similar to those of human beings; the Abnaki tribe of Quebec, on encountering the footprints of a bear, said that they had been made by their cousin. Furthermore, bears may often stand upright, a feature more characteristic of Man than animals, and also sometimes feed by passing food to their mouth using their paws, suggestive of a dexterity equal to that of the human hand. Also, the food that bears eat is similar to the types of food sought by Ancient hunter-gatherers; they even ate food in the same relative proportions, approximately 80 per cent vegetable matter and 20 per cent meat.

However, the most convincing factor of the kinship between bears and Man was probably the resemblance that the skinned corpse of a bear has to a human body; the Inuit tell stories of polar bears that become human when they 'take their coats off' as they enter a house, becoming bears once again when they put them back on to go outside.

The realization of such similarities can be seen in the way different tribes referred to the bear. The Ojibwa tribe of Ontario, for example, often referred to bears as *anijinabe*, their word for 'Indian', and the Yapavi people of Arizona said that bears are like people, except that they cannot make fire.

Another reason why native peoples so respected bears was because of the maternal devotion they display, epitomized in the fierce protection of cubs by their mother. Bears are born very much dependent on their mothers, especially black-bear and brown-bear cubs, born tiny, blind and virtually hairless in winter dens. For the first 3 months of life, all a cub knows is its mother and, on leaving the den, may stay with her for 2–3 years. The Ancient Roman writer, Pliny, believed that mother bears licked their cubs into shape; French mothers still refer to a badly behaved child as an *ours mal lechée* – 'a badly licked bear'. Early Greeks and Romans referred to bears only in the feminine gender, again reflecting a recognition of their strong maternal behaviour.

Most likely, the main reason that bears were held in such reverence was the mystery shrouding hibernation. Bears disappeared underground with the first heavy snowfall of the year, staying hidden there for up to 6 or 7

Bears commonly stand on their hind legs, assuming a rather human posture. This is possibly the origin of some of the beliefs that bears are actually human beings in another image.

months, neither eating, drinking nor passing wastes, finally to emerge only when the weather warmed up in spring. To early peoples this was seen as a miracle; they believed that the bear had died in winter and been reborn in spring. Furthermore, female bears often emerged with newly born cubs, which was regarded as even more marvellous since both birth and rebirth seem to have occurred.

Thus, the bear has become symbolic of birth and renewal, as indicated by the common use of words such as 'birth' and child 'bearing' throughout Europe; the verb 'to bear children' in German is *beran*, derived from the old European root 'bher'.

BEAR MOTHER

The *Bear Mother* story unites the ideas of the bear's similarity to human beings and its maternal devotion. Although there are many versions of this myth, it probably originated among Tsimshian peoples of northwestern North America and subsequently spread from there to other language groups, both in North America and Eurasia. The following is adapted from the most common account and closely resembles the original form of the tale:

> Peesunt, a young Indian woman, while out collecting berries with two other women of her tribe, was observed by some bears to be behaving in a noisy and disrespectful fashion. On her way back to the village she further offended the bears with coarse comments resulting from having slipped in some bear dung.
>
> With the strap of her carrying basket having broken, Peesunt found herself in difficulty when darkness fell, but was assisted by two young men wearing bear skins, who appeared out of the woods and took her to their home in the mountains. These young men turned out to be bears who had taken her with the intention of her becoming the wife of one of them. With death as her only alternative, she agreed, assuming high status among the 'spirit bears'. In time she gave birth to twins – half bear, half human.
>
> During the time of her absence, her family had been searching for her; with some assistance from Peesunt herself, her two brothers finally found her and slew her bear husband, but spared her two children. Before dying, the bear taught the brothers two ritual songs which they should sing over dead bears to ensure good luck. The families of these young men subsequently became prosperous bear-hunters, each adopting as their crest 'the Ensnared Bear'.

The bears of the story were not common animals but spirits which could hear blasphemy at great distances and which demanded respect. Being able to assume human form, they were mistaken by the woman for ordinary men; the woman herself then also became a spirit, giving birth to children that were able to change form at will. Bear-Mother's offspring acted as agents of goodwill between men and the powerful bear spirits, thus ensuring successful bear-hunting. As hunters came to realize that bears were part animal and part divinity, their hunting activities evolved into a more sacred enterprise.

Throughout its circumpolar distribution it is possible to identify certain central tenets within the *Bear Mother* tale: the mystic union between human being and spirit, the production of a chimeric offspring which acts as an intermediary between the two realms, and the requirement for ritualistic practices by which human representatives may converse with the spirit world. Additionally, the tale embodies the concept of divine altruism for human benefit.

The *Bear Mother* myth is a very common theme for illustration and can be seen on Tsimshian totem poles of the Skeena and Nass River areas and in the carvings of the northern Haida of Masset (Queen Charlotte Islands, Canada). It is also found to be a significant part of the culture of other peoples throughout the northern hemisphere. Sculptures dating back to the sixth and seventh millenium BC, unearthed in old Europe by Marija Gimbutas, also depict the *Bear Mother* theme. Many show a bear-headed woman seated on a throne decorated with crescents; often she is holding her left breast, emphasizing her role as a nurturing mother, in others she

Bears are commonly found on the totem poles of North American Indians, either as an illustration of the *Bear Mother* story or as the depiction of a clan crest.

is shown nursing a bear cub. Gimbutas called these terracotta figurines 'bear nurses'.

Directly connected to the *Bear Mother* myths are the tales of the Bear Son. The offspring of a human mother and bear god, Bear Son undergoes a series of heroic adventures, in which he is attacked by various monsters, while trying to establish his identity. Throughout his journey he becomes reconciled to his human nature and also gains enough insight into his divine origins to become responsible for both worlds. At the end of the journey he returns home to his adopted father and marries a princess whom he had rescued from the underworld.

THE BEAR AS A SYMBOL OF IMMORTALITY, REBIRTH AND RENEWAL

Observations of hibernating behaviour in bears gave rise to a belief in their rejuvenating powers and, from this, the legend of Salmoxis appears to have arisen. The Greek historian, Herodotus, writes of a Thracian cult centred around their God of Immortality, Salmoxis (literally 'bear skin'). One rite of this cult involved simulated death – fasting within a 'cave-like place' – and rebirth with the promise of immortality; another involved human sacrifice, the victim acting as a messenger to the god. By performing ritual sacrifices, people anticipated immortality.

The legend from which this cult arose tells how Salmoxis, born in Thrace and sold in slavery to Pythagoras, is later freed and, on returning to Thrace, started preaching to its people. He erected a large banqueting hall in which he held great feasts and preached that death is not an end and how 'neither himself nor his guests nor yet their children's children should die, but should come to stay in that very place and there should live forever in enjoyment of every happiness'. He then disappeared into an underground chamber and was mourned as dead. However, after 3 years, he reappeared to prove the truth of his teachings.

The Classicist, Rhys Carpenter believes that: 'Salmoxis can be none other than the hibernating bear, whose mysterious, foodless midwinter sleep has everywhere made of him a supernatural spirit to the wondering mind of primitive man'.

Among many native North American tribes there was a ceremonial association between hibernation and initiation. Initiation ceremonies were very widespread and used most frequently to bring children into adulthood; they were also used when welcoming adults into secret societies and in the initiation of shamans.

A common pattern underlaid each of these ceremonies; all involved prolonged isolation, fasting, symbolic death and rebirth, a pattern paralleling the bear in hibernation.

Often in manhood initiation rites either the initiate acted in the manner of a bear, or another person, impersonating a bear, appeared in the ceremony. The Dakota, a Sioux-speaking tribe of southern Minnesota, described initiation to manhood as 'making a bear'. The boy fasted for several days before the ceremony began; after this time, in a large cleared area away from the village, he erected a pole from which he hung a pipe (as a sacrifice) and a fawn skin painted with images from a dream which had signalled his readiness to become a man. He then dug a 'bear's hole' 200–300m (220–330yd) from the pole and made two paths cutting across it; around this he erected a brush enclosure. For the following 2 days the boy stayed in this 'den' and acted like a bear. On the last day of the retreat, young men from the village gathered together to 'kill the bear'. A dramatic fight ensued between the 'bear' and his attackers, ending finally in 'death', the body being carried like a corpse to a lodge (erected for the ritual) in which it was left, isolated from the rest of the camp. At sunset the youth emerged from the lodge as an adult.

The male initiation ceremony of the Eastern Pomo tribe of California involved a man impersonating a female grizzly bear. Dressed in a bear skin with raccoon skins representing bear cubs, the 'she-bear' charged up and down in front of a subterranean dance-house. One of the initiates was pushed into the path of the impersonator, who consequently knocked the youth down and did not allow him to get back up. The 'she-bear' then went into the dance-house, took off the bear skin, sat and smoked a pipe for a while, then put on the skin again and danced out. The following day further activities were carried out in which the initiates themselves imitated bears, after which there was a big feast and the boys were declared men.

Initiation for girls came with their first menstruation. Among the Ojibwa, girls were identified with the dangerous aspect of bears. Women were generally considered to be dangerous during their menstrual periods – the first one being the worst; an Ojibwa girl about to start her first menstruation was called *wemukowe* ('going to be a bear'). At the first sign of blood the girl was isolated from the rest of the village in a hut in the forest and was referred to as *mukowe* ('she is a bear'). In this case the bear is not only an initiation symbol but also represents the maleficent powers of the menstruating woman.

Initiation of adults into secret societies also centred on the symbolism of death and birth, as can be seen in the Midewiwin, or Medicine Lodge Society, of the Ojibwa. This was principally a healing society for both men and women which taught that, after death, they would be born into a new life in another realm. The Bear was the society's principal patron; all initiates were said to 'follow the bear path'. The origin myth for this ritual taught that the bear spirit, *Makwa Manido*, originally carried the Midewiwin doctrine of 'everlasting life' to the Ojibwa. The society comprised four levels, each requiring a new initiation involving more complex teachings. In some communities the society built special lodges for candidates entering the highest level. These lodges had two additional entrances; opposite each a small brush hut, known as a 'bear nest', was constructed. Just inside the lodge, on either side of the eastern and western entrances, red and black posts were set with a rock at the base of each. These posts represented the four limbs and feet of the bear spirit who, in the origin myth, created the four lodge entrances to the malevolent beings which opposed him; the bear rested in the nests after his struggle with these spirits. Candidates being initiated into the fourth degree walked like a bear up to each of the four entrances in turn and shot at the evil spirits inside with bows and arrows, after which they hurried back outside to hide in one of the 'nests'. Medicine bags of fourth-degree initiates were often made from bear paws or skins of bear cubs.

Central to the society was the belief that death was not an end, merely a passing from one world to another, a transition symbolized each time an initiate entered a new level and which was preparation for true death.

Shamanic initiation also revolved around death and resurrection. Here, initiates had to experience ordeals taking them to the limits of human endurance. Bears were involved, not only because they symbolized renewal, but also because they were considered very powerful spirits with which shamans would wish to be associated.

The bear's symbolization of renewal through hibernation formed a major part of the World Renewal Ceremony of the Munsee-Mahican Delaware tribe of Canada. Held on the day of the first new moon in January, this ritual ensured that the cycle of seasons would be maintained: a celebration of the unity of all creation and the renewal of the earth in spring. It intertwined three symbols of renewal: the bear, the moon and the World Tree.

The last Munsee-Mahican World Renewal Ceremony occurred in January 1850 on the Six Nations Reserve in Ontario. It took place in a large, east-west rectangular enclosure called *Xwate'k'an*, ('The Big House'), a representation of the universe. At the centre of this building was the trunk of a massive tree (the centre post) marking the centre of the world. Some authors believe that the positions occupied by ceremonial officials and the placement of furnishings corresponded to the positions of the stars forming the constellation Ursa Major. Actors performed the symbolic

This is the entrance to the community house of chief Shakes of the Tlingit people of the northwestern Pacific coast of North America. The entrance represents the vagina of the Bear Mother totem.

association between the motion of the stellar bear and the life cycle of its earthly counterpart.

The ceremony started with a woman who dreamed the location of a male bear in its den (the Delaware were prohibited from killing female bears). On the *Withke'katen*, ('Moon of the New Year') the woman told the chief and 12 selected hunters of her dream and the location of the bear. It was believed that the bear revealed its secret location to the woman so that it might, once again, be sacrificed to renew the earth. Once found, the bear was taken alive, guided back to the village and taken through the east door of the Big House to the base of the centre post, where it was killed by the chief with a single blow to its head. The chief then spoke to its spirit, instructing it to ascend the post and report to the sky beings that all was well on earth and that the ceremony had begun. It was believed that, during the course of the 12-day ceremony, the bear spirit climbed the World Tree to pass through the 12 layers of the heavens, carrying the message of the people to the creator – a prayer that the cycle of the seasons would continue, that there would be abundant plant and animal foods, and that the world would not depart from its ways. This rite marked the climax of the hunting season; it guaranteed the rebirth of animals killed during the hunt and a continued supply of meat.

Rites ensuring the return of life and the coming of spring also existed in Europe; again the bear was symbolic. In England such ceremonies were held on the first Monday after Epiphany (Plough Monday) and involved a man dressing up in straw to look like a bear and being led by young men from house to house to dance for money. In Germany and Czechoslovakia similar rites were held in late February or early March; again a man dressed in straw was led from door to door. In some communities he wore a bear mask, in others he dressed in a bear skin.

Another celebration of spring associated with the bear occurs on the second of February; in Austria, Poland and Hungary it is known as 'Bear's Day' and marks the miracle of the bear's return from death after its long winter absence. This date is also celebrated as the day when Persephone, the Greek maiden goddess of spring, returned from the Underworld, bringing with her lengthening days and abundant fields.

THE POWER OF THE BEAR

North American Indians generally believed that human beings were spiritually less powerful than animals and thus needed to gain more power to ensure success in hunting or food-gathering and also to avoid being killed in battle. Power could be obtained from any animal or mythological being; such power spirits were known as 'guardians' and many chose the bear spirit as their guardian. A young man obtained these guardians on initiation into adulthood, principally through dreams and visions, during which the spirit gave the youth instructions for making a medicine bundle (treated as a manifestation of the spirit itself) and bestowed a piece of its body to be kept and protected; it may also have taught a medicine song which could be used to call the spirit.

Guardian spirits could also be obtained in ways other than visions; some tribes believed that each person was born with a guardian, while others felt

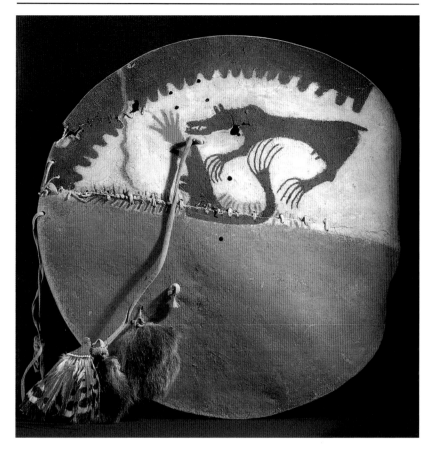

Many North American Indians possessed the bear spirit as a guardian obtained through visions. The bear guardian gave strength and ferocity during battle and was often depicted on war shields. The design on this Crow (plains) Indian shield depicts a female bear in an aggressive stance; the head of a second bear can also be seen emerging from the red portion of the shield.

that they were inherited from a deceased relative. Individuals belonging to tribes of the northern Great Plains were able to trade spirit guardians for valued material possessions, the grizzly-bear spirit often being traded as it was unpredictable and potentially dangerous. Most tribes considered the grizzly-bear spirit to be too powerful for women; some tribes even believed the grizzly to be too dangerous and unpredictable for anyone and actively avoided possessing them as guardians.

Nevertheless, many men (especially warriors and shamans) hoped to dream of this animal. Some tribes of the Great Plains and surrounding areas had exclusive societies made up of men, and occasionally women, who had bear spirits as guardians; these were known as 'Bear Cults'. During ceremonies they dressed themselves up as bears and refused to eat bear meat at feasts, instead eating berry soup. In battles they made bear-like noises, believing the power of the bear would protect them.

The considerable associations which existed between bears and shamans led to the belief that bears were the shamans of the animal world; many shamans possessed the bear as their guardian spirit. The carved staff, rattle and bear-claw crown shown here are parts of the equipment of Tsimshian shamans of the northwestern Pacific coast of North America.

Clans (kinships) within some tribes claim the bear as their totem, their belief being that they were descended from the original mythic being of the species. Individuals of the southeastern North American Yuchi Indian Bear Clan could not kill bears, an animal to which they prayed and danced at New Year and initiation ceremonies. Each Bear Clan member obtained protection from the bear and asked for its help when in trouble.

Another way in which some Indians derived power from the bear was by killing and eating part of the animal (usually the heart). After killing a grizzly, men of the Kwakitul tribe believed that they had assumed the bear's fishing ability, strength and ferocity. However, by this act, Man did not ask for the animal's power, but rather took it by force and, consequently, did not obtain a lifetime relationship with it.

Due to its power, many hunting tribes thought of the bear as the shaman of the animal kingdom. It was believed that bears, like shamans, could fore-tell the future and the belief that shamans could transform themselves into

The association between bears and shamans extended to other peoples also; this bronze plaque was used in shamanic rituals in the former USSR.

bears was widespread. That the two were associated stems from the similar roles they played in native North American hunting-cultures; they both served as a messenger to the 'Owner of the Animals' in the quest for game and, consequently, both were consulted about the prospects of future hunts. In addition both had healing powers and thus were both conceived as spiritually powerful, and potentially dangerous, entities.

The shaman, like the bear, lived in isolation in order to seek wisdom. Naturally, many shamans possessed bears as spirit helpers; these men dressed and painted themselves to look like bears and, in their medicine bundles, kept bear claws, teeth and other parts of the animal, which were used in their ceremonies. They sang power songs to the animal and they danced in the manner they believed bears to dance.

The Tunit, an Ancient people of the North American Arctic, were accomplished artists, carving tiny figurines from ivory, which are now known as 'Dorset art'. One such statuette depicts a bear, apparently in flight, incised with a stylized skeleton; in its neck was a tiny compartment with a sliding cover which may have held red ochre. It is thought to depict the spirit helper of an Inuit shaman, an *angakoq*; it was believed this spirit helper (or *tornait*) could take the *angakoq* to the moon or the bottom of the sea, in order to seek help from the goddess Sedna, who governed the whales, seals and walruses.

Not all bear-shamans used their special powers for the benefit of others; many were believed to be malevolent and dressed up as bears in order to murder and thieve. The Pomo Indians of central California called these 'wicked' shamans *gauk burakal* (literally 'human bear'); similarly, the Ojibwa called them 'bear walks'.

THE HEALING POWERS OF THE BEAR

The healing association between shamans and bears led the Pueblo Indians of southwestern North America to use the same name for their shamans who healed the sick as they used for the bear. Shamans did not depend on the therapeutic effects of plants to treat the sick, relying instead on their spirit helpers; they drew on the bear's spirit to effect cures and imitated bears during their curative rites.

Shamans were usually not the only healers in a tribe; very often there was also a medicine man or woman (or even a medicine society). Such medicine people were known as 'Master Gatherers' and likened to bears because of their knowledge of plants; a bear was considered to know a lot about plants by virtue of the fact that they formed a large part of its diet. (Many plants are in fact named after the bear – bearberry, bear clover, bear grass, bear huckleberry and bearwood, for instance – partly because, in the myths and tales of many tribes, it is the bear that first discovers the plant and then offers knowledge of it to the people.) Some of the plants that bears eat were medicines used by the tribe, their healing properties communicated to the healer by the bear. The Lakota Sioux believed that any man who dreamed of the bear would become an expert in the use of plant medicines; during their curative rites, songs were sung which made reference to the bear.

> My paw is sacred,
>   the herbs are everywhere.
> My paw is sacred,
>   all things are sacred.

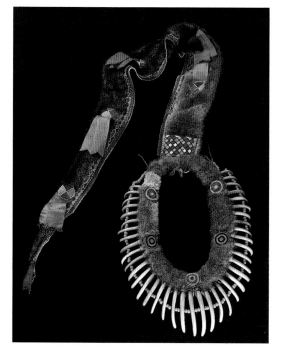

The bear-spirit guardian was both dangerous and unpredictable; accessible only to the bravest. This Fox (plains) Indian necklace is made of bear claws and was a mark of distinction for the wearer.

Pueblo Indian doctors drew power from the bear by wearing a bear-claw necklace and bear paws over their hands; often, they ate a plant known as 'bear root' to induce a trance-like state in order to diagnose an illness. Shamans of the Tlingit tribe of southeastern Alaska wore a bear-claw head-dress, touching the claws to the body of the patient to induce healing; the sound of the claws rattling together was believed to summon the healing bear spirits. Many plains tribes danced while imitating bears to gain personal power in order to cure the ailing.

BEAR DANCES

Bear dances of native North Americans were not performed exclusively to heal the sick; they were included as part of many ceremonies and were performed for a great number of reasons, e.g. bringing in the spring, ensuring an abundance of food over the coming year, guaranteeing protection from the bear and also providing protection from other men in battle. Some Indians danced while sacred objects were being transferred from one person to another and others danced simply to honour the bear as it emerged from its den after the long winter sleep.

It was a common belief that real bears did actually dance and, consequently, the dancers mimicked the way it was believed that bears moved. It was a Pawnee belief that bears danced by standing on their hind legs, lifting their paws towards the sun, and that it was in this way that the animals received their curative powers.

Some North American Indians performed bear-dances in which the movements of bears were mimicked. This usually involved donning a mask and the skin of a bear such as these used by Kwakiutl Indians of northwestern Canada.

As well as incorporating bear movements, the dances were often re-enactments of events which were believed to have taken place at the beginning of time. Sometimes, however, they were less serious and involved some clowning around, the dancers mimicking the comical antics of bears. Generally, in the western part of North America, where grizzlies occur, the dances were more serious, and sometimes even violent, as the imposing bear was being portrayed. In the east, where only black bears occur, comical dances were much more common.

Bear-dancers very often dressed up in bear skins and wore masks and bear-claw necklaces; some even put bear canines in their mouths to further impersonate bears. It is probable that both bear-dancers and spectators, believed that they became what they portrayed.

BEAR CEREMONIALISM

Many ancient tribes, both of North America and Eurasia, were enthusiastic and sophisticated bear-hunters who relished bear meat. However, some tribes killed bears only when left no other choice. Indians of southwestern North America allowed the killing of bears only when they attacked domestic stock, when medicine, such as bear paws, was needed for cere-mony, or when people were starving. The Navajo believed that to kill a bear under any other circumstance would lead to insanity; the Pima believed that bears caused bloating disease, and the Pueblos saw bears as transformed people and believed that they could make you sick. Such beliefs were usually attached to grizzly bears; these tribes had no fear of killing black bears, which were considered spiritually weak, unlike the larger and more danger-ous grizzly. This is illustrated by the fact that the Blackfoot word for black bear is *kyaio* ('bear') while their word for grizzly is *nitakyaio* ('real bear').

For those tribes which did hunt bears, specific rituals and taboos were adhered to before, during and after killing the animal. Similar rituals are observed all across the northern hemisphere and are believed to have originated within the hunting tribes of Asia, spreading as these tribes followed their game across the continent and into North America.

Among many peoples the hunt began with divination rites, used together with dreams; these predicted the outcome of the hunt. Both involved communication with the spirits which 'owned' the animals (it was believed that, when people dreamed, their souls left their bodies to travel in the spirit realm, from where they could see things otherwise invisible). A hunter may do several things in order to attract the right kind of dreams: put bear grease in his hair and bear patelles (dream charms) around his bed at night. It was believed that, if the animal killed was respected and all taboos observed, then the 'owner' of the animal would be pleased and inclined to release more. Once free, these animals themselves could choose whether or not to be killed.

The most important part of this divination was to locate the bear den and was thus carried out in autumn, when the bear had just entered hibernation. However, hunts did not usually take place until the beginning of spring, when food stores were at their lowest.

It was customary among North American tribes for individual hunters to take the most direct routes to dens without following the tracks of any other animal; this would be considered 'unfaithful' to the bear. The Ancient Lapps, however, hunted bears in groups, and marched to the den in a predetermined order. The hunter who had discovered the location of the den in the previous autumn took the lead, followed by a 'drumbeater' who, in turn, was followed by the man who was going to make the first attack.

All primitive hunting tribes observed strict taboos over which weapons could be used to kill the animal. It was generally believed that bears should be given a 'fair fight' and only archaic weapons could be used; striking or thrusting weapons meant both hunter and hunted were more evenly matched. It was also believed by some tribes that modern firearms were not 'strong enough' for such a spiritually powerful beast. Most tribes used a spear or an axe.

There were three main methods generally employed for killing bears; the most common was to force a bear out of its lair by shouting or provoking it with a spear and, as it emerged, attacking it with spears, axe or bow-and-arrow. Alternatively, the bear might be attacked in the open by a group of hunters (or even one on his own); again, the weapon used was usually a spear. The third method involved trapping, either using snares (causing death by choking), or deadfalls (comprising logs which pinned or crushed the animal).

Direct reference to the bear was never made before, during or after the hunt; special names were used to honour the animal and placate its spirit. Many such names are kinship terms, most commonly 'Grandfather' or 'Grandmother' are used but also 'Cousin' (Abenaki Indians), 'Beloved Uncle', 'Good Father' (Ural-Altaic peoples), 'Uncle of the Woods' (Votyak), 'Great Father' and 'Little Uncle' (Indo-European). Other names were based on some real or imaginary characteristic of the bear: 'The One Who Owns the Chin' (Montagnais-Naskapi Indians), 'Black Food', 'Short-Tail' (Montagnais-Naskapi and Eastern Cree), 'Crooked Tail' (Eastern Cree), 'Four-legged Human' (plains Cree), 'Honey Paws', 'Forest-Apple' and

Bears were held in great respect and the hunting of these animals usually observed strict taboos, principal among which was the use of archaic weapons. This Inuit arrowshaft-straightener is carved from walrus ivory and is in the form of a bear; it is engraved with depictions of shamans and animals.

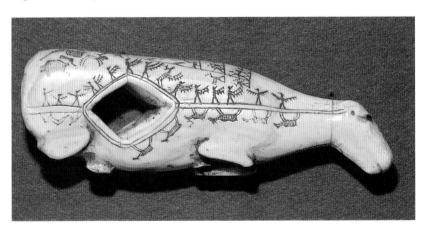

'Famous Light-foot' (Finns) and 'Golden Feet' (Indo-European). Some-times bears were referred to metaphorically, e.g. 'dear little divine thing who resides among the mountains' (Ainu), 'Golden Friend of the Fen and Forest', 'Loved-One from the Glenwood' (Finns) and 'Venerable One' (Voguls).

Usually, different names were used to refer to the bear at different times; for instance, the Montagnais-Naskapi referred to it before the hunt by its generic, *macke'w*, while in the woods they call it 'Black Food'. When the bear was in its den they called it 'Grandfather' or 'Grandmother' but, after its death, they again referred to it as 'Black Food'.

Athapaskan Indians of Alaska spoke about bears using riddles. A hunter, finding a bear in its den, communicated the information by means of gestures, *gwizhii ideegwidhi* ('wisdom that is performed') or verbally, *gwizhii ideeridlii* ('wisdom that is told'). For instance, he may have walked clumsily in imitation of the bear or, on being offered food, may have asked where the accompanying fat and grease were. Both, however, were oblique; no direct reference to the animal was made as it was believed that bears could understand human speech, hear over great distances and would be angered by the use of their name. Additionally, it was believed that it would be bad luck for women and children to know that a bear had been found; by speaking in riddles, which only the men understood, hunters were able to conceal their discovery.

Names of reverence were also commonly used when coaxing the bear out of its den. Many tribes requested that the bear allow itself to be killed. After the bear had been killed (and sometimes before), these special names were used in speeches which served to apologize to the bear and appease its soul. North American Indians made speeches that praised the bear and explained why they had killed it. The Lillooet Indians of southern British Columbia, Canada, chanted a special song over the body of the bear which named the boons of power they expected to derive from slaying him:

> You were the first to die, greatest of beasts.
> We respect you and shall treat you accordingly;
> > No woman will eat your flesh,
> > No dog insult you.
> May the lesser animals all follow you
> > And die by our traps and arrows.
> May we now kill plenty of game.
>
> May the goods of those we gamble with
> > Follow us as we leave the play,
> > And come into our possession.
> May the goods of those we play lehol with
> > Become completely ours,
> > Even as a beast that we have slain.

Apologetic speeches of tribes of northern Siberia usually included a state-ment disclaiming responsibility, blaming instead the Russians. The Finns also disclaimed responsibility, as illustrated by a verse from the Finnish folk epic, *The Kalevala* ('The Land of Heroes'). The hero of the song is the old magician, Vainamoinen, who sings out after the bear has been slain:

O my Otso, O my darling,
Fair one with the paws of honey,
Be not filled with causeless anger,
I myself have not o'erthrown thee,
Thou thyself have left the forest,
Wandered from thy pine-tree covert,
Thou hast torn away thy clothing,
Ripped thy grey cloak in the thicket.

After conciliatory speeches had been made, various rites were performed on the body of the bear, which again served to appease the spiritual controller, ensuring a regular supply of similar game. Most commonly, tobacco was placed in the bear's mouth, the hunter sitting down and smoking next to the bear. Common in North America was the use of the *nimaban*, or 'dance-cord', a string of tanned moose hide bearing symbolic decoration. This was placed on the chest or about the neck and was used to carry the bear back to camp; if the bear had to be left in the woods, it was believed that this would protect the carcass from scavenging by other predators.

When the bear was brought back to camp, there were often specific taboos to be observed, most commonly concerning women. Young girls and married women without children of the Montagnais-Naskapi Indians were required to retreat to a dwelling which they had built themselves some distance from the rest of the camp. Unmarried women of the Mistassini had to cover their faces; only married women could assist in skinning the carcass. Ostyak and Vogul women of western Siberia also had to cover their faces and hide their hands so that the bear could not see any uncovered part of their body. Furthermore, they were forbidden to look the bear in the eye or kiss its lips. Girls and childless women of the Ancient Micmac were forbidden to enter the wigwam when the bear was being eaten; this was also true of Ancient Lapps. The men of the Tungus people of central Siberia forbade the presence of women entirely.

The bear was often taken to a specific dwelling, either especially erected or the home of the hunter; the body often being carried through some opening other than the ordinary doorway. The Ainu of Hokkaido, Japan, called this special entrance, *kamui kush puyara* ('the window through which divine beings pass'). Lapp hunters would announce their arrival by pounding three times on their door shouting 'sacred man' if the bear was male, or, if female, 'sacred virgin'. Some suggest that this practice was not intended to announce the killing but to magically transfer the power and strength of the dead bear to the hunter's household.

Specific rituals attended skinning, cooking and eating the bear. Mistassini Indians would slit the skin from the throat downwards, thus distinguishing it from other animals, on which the reverse cut was used, and signifying high regard. Among Lapps, the bear-slayer performed the flaying; first he cut off the skin of the nose and fastened this to his own face; the skin of the head, however, was never removed. It was customary for the bear to be dressed before being eaten. The Nootka and Kwakitul Indians of the North Pacific coast area treated the bear as an honoured guest, sitting it in an upright posture and inviting it to eat from a tray set before it. The Asiatic Eskimo of northeastern Siberia offered food to the skin of the bear (head and shoulders still attached) before it entered the house, where it was placed on the master's side of the sleeping-room, a place of honour, for 5 days and nights. During this time it was decorated with beads and offered sacrifices. Loud noise was avoided lest the bear be woken; it was accompanied at all times so that it should not 'feel lonely'. The Ostyak and Vogul skinned the animal, leaving the head and forepaws intact; these were then placed on a wooden table and positioned so that the chin lay between the paws. They placed images of deer made of bread or birch bark before it; on its eyes they placed silver coins and to its chin they fixed a birch bark 'muzzle', preventing women looking it in the eyes or kissing its lips. If the bear were female, rings were placed on its claws.

The Ancient Lapps boiled the blood of the bear with some of its fat; this was drunk as a toast to the animal before the meat was touched. Some Inuit hung small parts of the bear, attached to objects such as knives and saws, in their huts as gifts to the bear's soul. These were left for 3 days, after which, it was believed, the soul would tell other bears how well it had been treated so that they would also be willing to be caught. The Montagnais-Naskapi Indians cooked the bear meat simultaneously in two separate kettles, the contents of each being eaten separately. Men and older women attended the first repast and, once the women had left, the men were required to eat all that remained. This 'eat all' feature was a common theme in many bear ceremonies. Penobscot Indians roasted the bear whole whereas northern Algonquians burnt certain parts of the animal, in order to feed the spirit of the bear; parts of the heart were so burnt, the hunter eating the remainder in order to imbibe the 'cunning and courage of his victim'. The women were forbidden to eat the head or paws and men, the rump. The Nootka boiled the flesh and entrails into a soup and ate every part of the animal except the belly. Men of the Ostyak and Vogul peoples of north western Siberia eat the head, heart and paws in the woods, women cooking and eating the hindquarters in the village.

Almost invariably, festivities lasting a few days surrounded the killing of a bear and the eating of its flesh. Very often this included a ritual enactment of the *Bear Mother* story, Ostyaks and Voguls also acted out the story of Konsyg-Oik ('Old-Clawed One'), who they believe to have been the first bear. This story tells how Konsyg-Oik begged his father, Great Torum (the highest deity), with whom he lived in the stars, to let him go down to earth. Torum agreed and gave him a bow-and-arrow and fire, but would not let him back until he had established law and order on earth. Konsyg-Oik, however, created a lot of trouble among men, whereupon one of seven human brothers killed him, took away his bow-and-arrow and the fire and gave them to humankind. During the festival, dancers portrayed how the first bear was stalked and ambushed and how seven arrows were needed to bring him down. The descendants of the Ostyaks and Voguls, now known as the Khanty and Mansi, still hold this bear festival at the end of winter, when a hunter has killed a bear.

The last aspect of ceremonial ritualism involved disposing of the remains. Most Ancient peoples of the northern hemisphere placed the skull in the woods, either hanging it from a tree branch or pole, or burying it in the ground at a sacred spot. The remaining bones were disposed of in various ways; Menomini Indians wrapped them with tobacco and threw them into

Nearly all parts of a hunted bear were put to some use. This metal knife is of Blackfoot design; the hilt is a bear jaw.

a river. It was a general belief that dogs should be kept away from these bones; the dog's 'spirit' was thought to offend the 'owner' of the animals, which would result in bad luck in hunting.

THE AINU AND THE GILYAK

To the Ainu and Gilyak of eastern Asia, bear ceremonies had special meaning. The Gilyak people of Siberia believed that natural features of the earth and heavens and members of the animal kingdom all had spiritual 'owners' or 'masters' for which the visible, physical aspect was merely appearance. Such supernatural beings were believed to control the stock of game and fish on which the people's livelihood depended. It was believed that the souls of deceased Gilyak became associated with these 'owners' should they drown or be killed by wild animals. Thus, the soul of a Gilyak killed by a bear became a 'little owner', having a special relationship with the 'owner' of the bear. These deceased Gilyak became special supernatural protectors of their living relatives, linking the supernatural and earthly realms by the closest bonds of fellowship. Thus, homage was rendered by living Gilyak to their deceased relatives as well as the supernatural 'owners' by means of sacrifice and festivals held in their honour; the bear festival was one of the most important.

The Gilyak looked upon bears as honoured emissaries from the supernatural realm. After one was ceremonially killed its soul was believed to return to the supernatural world as a messenger. The slaughter of the animal was thus an occasion for making offerings to the 'owners'; in return, the latter provided a ready supply of game. It was essential to venerate the slain bear, which might be a member of the 'mountain-spirit fraternity' or an incarnation of some clansman's spirit received into that fraternity.

The Ainu of Hokkaido, Japan, believed that the 'owner' of the mountain was the 'master' of bears; on one hand he was a man, on the other a bear (of unusually large size) and all bears were his fellow tribesmen. The Ainu, of course, only came into direct contact with living bears but, because of the association of these beasts with one of the most important 'masters', a being believed to control an large part of their food supply, bears were treated with greatest respect. Slaughter of a bear enables the passage of the animal's soul to its 'master' and subsequent return to earth, completing a cycle of considerable importance to the Ainu mind. *Iomante*, the Ainu word for 'sacrifice', means literally 'to send away'.

Both Ainu and Gilyak captured sacrificial bears as young cubs, treated them as honoured guests for 2 to 3 years, even, in some cases, to the extent of being suckled by the wife of the hunter when very young. When the time came for the sacrifice the animal was removed from its cage, tied with a rope and led about, either to various houses or just within a circle of people. Along the way it was teased and provoked to make it angry. It was finally led and tethered to a decorated stake. Two men took hold of the back legs and two others the front; two poles for strangling were held on either side of the neck. A marksman shot an arrow into the heart in such a way that no blood spilled to the earth, the poles were then squeezed together to hasten death and the 'little guest' was gone.

The body of the bear, or sometimes just the hide with the head attached, was then decorated with charms and offered food and drink. It may then have been honoured with a speech beseeching it to return directly to the spirit world and relate how well it had been cared for.

A celebratory feast then followed; the head of the bear was separated from the rest of the pelt and placed on a pole (called *ke-omande-ni*, 'the pole for sending away'). The festival continued until every bit of the 'little god' had been consumed.

THE CULT OF ARTEMIS

In Classical times the goddess Artemis was identified with the bear through-out the European continent, where it was considered sacred to her. In one of her forms (Atalanta) she was cared for and nursed in her infancy by a she-bear. Some Classical scholars identify her mother as Demeter, whose name translates as 'grain of the bear mother'.

Artemis was the 'lady of wild nature', present everywhere in mountains and fields; she was considered the protectress of animals, women in childbirth and all little children. She ruled the plants and the growth and regeneration of vegetation and annually died to be reborn next spring, analogous to the bear emerging from hibernation. However, also like a bear, she had a dark side – the devouring terrible mother and a destroyer demanding animal sacrifices, her wrath causing women to die in childbirth.

In Classical Greece, it was a prerequisite of marriage that girls be initiated in a rite called *arkteia*. The girls had to undergo a period of seclusion outside the city, in an isolated sanctuary of Artemis. During their segregation the girls, known as *arktoi*, or 'she-bears', were said to have behaved like the animal. The girls also participated in a feast dedicated to Artemis, where they danced the *arkteuin* ('acting the she-bear'), wearing brown robes in imitation of bear cubs.

The Celtic counterpart of Artemis was the bear goddess, Artio, an image of whom was found at Bern ('bear city'), the coat-of-arms of which shows a

This ninth-century Pictish stone slab from Perthshire, Scotland, shows that the bear was still held in high regard at this time. The slab depicts a Celtic horned god with a bear and a wolf or otter.

British Celts also saw the bear as a cult animal. This bear cameo was excavated at South Shields (Tyne and Wear) and dates from about the third century AD.

bear. The name Arthur derives from the Celtic verbal root, 'art' ('bear'); the legendary warrior king of this name is often depicted as being asleep in an underground tomb, waiting to be awakened, at which point the country will be returned to prosperity. This is possibly a literary analogy to the bear in hibernation and its emergence heralding spring.

HEAVENLY BEARS

Two clusters of bright stars dominate the heavens in the northern hemisphere; they are known from Classical mythology as the Great Bear – 'Ursa Major' – and the Little Bear – 'Ursa Minor'. The Pole Star, 'the hub around which the heavens turn', is at the end of the Little Bear's tail and it is possible 'to get one's bearings' by sighting on the first two stars of Ursa Minor, which point directly to the Pole Star; the nearby Great Bear also offers sighting lines by which it can be found.

To the Greeks these stars represented Callisto, an attendant of Artemis, who had taken a vow of chastity, and her son, Arcas. In one version of the story, the god Zeus seduced and impregnated the pure Callisto. When Hera, the wife of Zeus, heard of this, she transformed the young girl into a bear and tricked Artemis into killing her. Zeus, after hearing of Callisto's death, set her among the constellations as the Great Bear and ensured the safety of their son, Arcas, by providing a refuge for him on Mount Kyllene. When Hera found Callisto among the stars she was angered further and used her powers to ensure that the constellation revolved ceaselessly around the Pole Star. When Arcas, too, was killed, Zeus set him in the sky, as the Little Bear, to be his mother's eternal guardian.

According to Hindu mythology, the Great Bear is a masculine force that keeps the universe continually whirling, both profitably and disastrously, as he controls the seasons and the weather, thus determining the crop production. He is also believed to safeguard the passage of a child from the womb.

The Inuit believe that these stars represent a bear being continually chased by a pack of dogs, in remembrance of a woman who betrayed a family of bears by revealing the location of their dwelling to her husband. One of the angered bears set out to punish the woman but, in so doing, was set upon by her husband's dogs; during the ensuing fight between the bear and the dogs, a great fire descended from the sky, engulfed them and returned them to the sky as the Great Bear and pursuing Little Bear.

Throughout the northern hemisphere, these two constellations are repeatedly perceived as bears, a remarkable fact considering that many cultures were isolated from one another for considerable amounts of time.

THE CHANGING IMAGE OF THE BEAR

Early Western writings still appeared to revere the bear. After studying Homer's Greek epic, *The Odyssey* (*c.*700 BC), Rhys Carpenter argues that the hero, Odysseus, is modelled on the older hero, the Bear Son. In fact, the Bear Son theme is carried right through to the eighth century AD and appears in the first substantial work of literature in English, the poem, 'Beowulf'. The name of the hero translates as 'Bee-Wolf', which in turn means 'bear', and the poem depicts Beowulf undergoing the same adventures as the Bear Son himself.

Icelandic sagas of the seventh and eighth centuries AD featured warriors known as 'Berserkers'; 'ber' derives from the root word meaning 'bear' and 'serk' means 'shirt'. These warriors summoned up bear courage and protection from the bear spirits by wearing a bear skin; some warriors were even said to change into bear form when the fighting turned particularly fierce. Thus, at this time, the bear was still revered as a symbol of strength and honour.

By the Middle Ages, however, the image of the bear had begun to change; the *Reynard Cycle*, of Flemish, German and French origin, published in the thirteenth century, depicts the bear as greedy and gluttonous; *Aesop's Fables* characterized the bear, Bruno, as stupid and vulnerable to deception, paving the way for folk tales which often pitted the gullible bear against the wily fox. All such tales emphasized that it was the bear's greed and tendency to sleep a lot that made it such a slow thinker. In some of these tales, the bear, in addition to characterizing sloth and greed, was also used to illustrate the sinfulness of lust and fornification.

It was during the Middle Ages that the Church decided to adopt the animal; the female bear was compared to the Virgin Mary in recognition of its material devotion and the fact that the cub is born during hibernation, giving the appearance of an immaculate conception. The male bear was also adopted by the Christians, but as a representation of the unconverted pagan, able finally to be domesticated by the Church. Many of the earliest saints of the Church were portrayed as having tamed the animal; consequently some of these saints made the bear their mascot. The Middle Ages/Renaissance poem, 'The Masquerade of Orson and Valentine', illustrates this taming process: twin boys are abandoned in a forest; one manages to find his way to King Pippin's court, where he is named Valentine (a name which embodies the idea of Christian love); the other is left in the forest and is raised by bears. Many years later, the two brothers encounter one another; Valentine tames his twin using the power of love and names him Orson, so that he will not forget his bestial upbringing and so remain grateful for his salvation.

The nineteenth-century fairy tale of *Goldilocks*, in which bears are depicted as both homely and fierce, tells of how a young girl (an old woman in the original version) is inadvertently attracted to the food, warmth and comfort of a bear family's home, from which she has to escape on the animals' return. It is possible that such stories, and similarly the stories of *Little Red Riding Hood*, were created in order to prevent children wandering into areas inhabited by dangerous wild animals.

At the beginning of the twentieth century, the bear's image once again changed, largely due to the creation of the teddy bear in 1902. In November of that year, the President of the USA, Theodore Roosevelt, went to Mississippi to help settle a boundary dispute. During his stay he took part in some hunting; one version of the story tells that he had little success and so a black bear cub was brought out on a lead for him to shoot. Because of its small size and the circumstances the President refused to shoot it, saying: 'I draw the line. If I shot that little fellow, I couldn't look my own boys in the face again'. Cartoon images of this event soon appeared in newspapers, and a small toy bear was offered for sale next to a copy of the cartoon. The bear, first known as 'Teddy's bear' was an instant success and has since become one of the most popular toys ever made.

Another boost to the bear's image came in the form of the USA's 'Smokey the Bear'. Smokey was created during World War 2 as an educational aid in the prevention of forest fires; his image became a familiar friend and, in the 1950s, the Smokey Bear Act was passed in order to protect this image by law.

Today the bear is still a popular image; six US states use it as an emblem and California has even made the grizzly its official state animal. Popular bear characterizations abound in cartoon imagery, depicting them as intelligent (Rupert Bear), cunning (Yogi Bear), accident prone (Barney Bear), somewhat dull-witted (Winnie-the-Pooh), and, in possibly the most famous cartoon bear, as the epitome of the 'laid-back', West-Coast surfer (Baloo, in Walt Disney's *The Jungle Book*). Although the charactistic depiction alters, the fact remains that bears are one of the most popular cartoon figures, a reflection of the ubiquitous, deep sense of familiarity we have for this animal.

Chapter 2
Classification, Form and Function

The order Carnivora, to which the bears belong, is defined by zoologists on the basis not of a carnivorous life-style, but rather on dental specializations which demonstrate the collective affinity of the various members of the order. During the evolutionary history of the group, eight terrestrial and three aquatic families have arisen at various times. Although, strictly, all of these may be grouped together, it is traditionally accepted that the aquatic families (eared seals – Otariidae; true seals – Phocidae; Walrus – Odobenidae) be considered separately as the order Pinnipedia. The order Carnivora is thus usually reserved to describe the terrestrial families (alternatively termed the order Fissipedia by some). It contains some 240 species, although the precise number varies as new species are discovered, subspecies are promoted to full species status, or previously recognized species come to be regarded as subspecies; occasionally species are also considered to have become extinct.

Carnivores have naturally distributed themselves across the globe on all continents except Antarctica, Australia, New Guinea, New Zealand and a number of small oceanic islands. However, on most of these exceptions, carnivores are nowadays present as a result of accidental or intentional introduction by Man. Stoats and mongooses now threaten ground-nesting birds on New Zealand and Hawaii; domestic cats are a hazard to penguin nurseries on some sub-Antarctic islands; and the dingo is a feral form of domestic dog introduced to Australia by Man some 4,000 years ago.

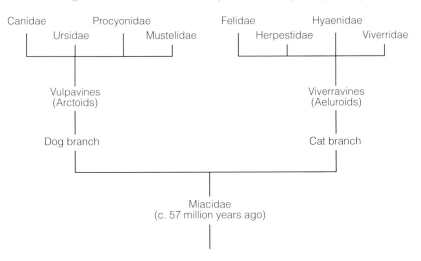

The family tree of the living Carnivora, all derived from the extinct family Miacidae.

The (terrestrial) Carnivora are divided into two superfamilies. The first, the Aeluroidea, is the cat branch of the order and contains the cats (Felidae), hyaenas (Hyaenidae), civets and genets (Viverridae) and mongooses (Herpestidae). The second superfamily, the Arctoidea, is the dog branch and comprises the dogs (Canidae), raccoons (Procyonidae), stoats and weasels (Mustelidae) and bears (Ursidae). These superfamilies represent an evolutionary divergence of these animals early in the history of the group, which is also represented by a basic difference in the distribution of their members, although this has subsequently been confused by individual species migrating into new areas. Nonetheless, it is possible to see that the arctoid carnivores originated in the New World whereas the aeluroids originated in the Old World. The alteration of the relative positions of the continental plates through geological time has since allowed animals to redistribute themselves and, in most families, such opportunities have been taken. However, apart from the red panda (*Ailurus fulgens*), there are no Old World procyonids; similarly, there are no New World hyaenids today (although there have been during the evolution of the group).

The smallest of the living carnivores is the least weasel (*Mustela nivalis*) which may measure a mere 17cm (7in) or so from nose to tail tip and weigh only 35g (1¼oz). At the other end of the scale is the polar bear (*Ursus maritimus*), measuring more than 2.5m (8¼ft) in length and weighing about 600kg (1,323lb). Members of the order also demonstrate a correspondingly large range of body forms, life-styles and life histories, so much so that it is not immediately obvious why zoologists place all of these diverse animals together in a single group.

Taxonomy is the branch of biology concerned with making sense of the vast array of life forms with which we find ourselves surrounded. This objective is achieved by compartmentalizing animals (and plants) into recognizable groups, members of which share common evolutionary origins. It is hardly surprising to find that taxonomy is often viewed as a rather esoteric discipline and the set of formalized rules to which taxonomists adhere, and the methods that they employ in order to derive their groupings, are complex. However, the basic rationale to which they work is quite simple: in evolutionary terms, any particular species will be more closely related to some species than it will be to others (in the same way that we are more closely related to our parents than to our cousins, next-door neighbours and work-mates, for instance). Clues to the nature of these relationships may be found in fossils and in the skeletal and dental morphology of the living species. As we shall come to see, life is not always this simple and different scientists tease apart the threads of these stories differently, often coming to quite disparate conclusions.

Nonetheless, it is to be expected that there should be a number of features common to all members of the Carnivora (or any other group) and, indeed, this is the case. In fact, when considering the Carnivora, only a single, diagnostic feature is necessary in order to recognize an animal as belonging to this group – on each side of the jaw the last upper premolar (P^4) and the first lower molar (M_1) have become modified by the development of blade-like extensions which shear against one another as the jaw closes; these are known as the *carnassial teeth*. Although this type of dental scissor, perfect for dealing with flesh, has also evolved in certain

Fur seals (above) and sea-lions are members of the Otariidae, a group which seems to have evolved from within the Ursidae some 30–27 million years ago.

other animals, in none of these other cases were these particular teeth employed.

Paradoxically however, not all *extant* (living) species of the group possess these teeth; some members of the Carnivora have, over the course of evolutionary time, abandoned their reliance on a diet of flesh and, in such cases, the carnassial teeth have become redundant. Although in some such species these teeth have merely been reduced, in others the new diet has required a new form of tooth and the shearing blades have been lost altogether. These animals are nonetheless still included in the Carnivora since they are known to have descended from species which did possess these specialized teeth. Clearly, the business of constructing taxonomic groups is complicated by changes which occur over time and which obscure diagnostically important characters. A good understanding of the fossil history of the species under consideration is important; the absence of such knowledge has, in the past, led to the proposition of some rather strange associations.

Terrestrial carnivores also possess a number of other basically common features. All have four or five, clawed digits on each limb; the first of these digits is not opposable (as it is in Man) and, in some cases, has become very small, while, in others, it has been reduced almost to the point of having been lost altogether. All bears have 5 digits on each limb, each with a strong, curved claw; these claws, like those of dogs, cannot be retracted in the way that most cats' claws can. One feature which has created some confusion in the past regarding the classification of the giant panda (*Ailuropoda melanoleuca*) is the presence of an extra, opposable digit on the hand, often referred to as the 'panda's thumb' (or radial sesamoid). This extra digit, however, is not really a thumb at all and has no bony, skeletal elements but consists of a horny pad of skin overlying a sesamoid structure (a structure produced in association with muscle tendon as opposed to being a mesenchymal derivative – which is the case for true bone) that has merely the appearance of a thumb.

Most Carnivora walk on the tips of their toes (digitigrade gait) and, in so doing, improve their running efficiency by increasing the length of their stride. Bears, on the other hand, walk on the soles of their feet rather like we do (plantigrade gait). This is quite rare among mammals in general and, together with the impression made by the claws, makes bear tracks quite unmistakable.

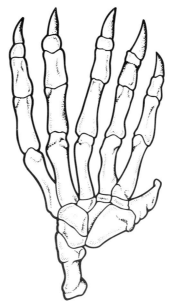

The false thumb (radial sesamoid) of the giant panda is a skeletal accessory structure which allows for efficient manipulation of bamboo. A similar structure is found in red pandas, another animal very dependent on bamboo for food.

Bears have very long claws, which are not retractile as they are in certain other carnivores. They are therefore evident in the tracks.

Bears walk on the soles of their feet and thus leave very distinctive tracks showing the sole of the foot and the length of the claws in mud or snow.

In relation to their body size, all carnivores have a large skull, a considerable portion of which surrounds the brain, reflecting the high degree of sensory acuity and 'intelligence' possessed by these animals – essential prerequisites of variously social and co-operatively-hunting species. The articulation of the jaw with the braincase permits only opening and closing movements; there is a very limited facility for the side-to-side movements, seen, for example, among the antelopes. This again demonstrates the basic dietary dependence on flesh, a food which can be sheared off in lumps and swallowed without chewing. Associated with the jaw articulation are very strong facial muscles, necessary for producing the powerful bite in which considerable force is exerted across the carnassial teeth. In some cases this is not only used for shearing off food but also for the delivery of a strong, killing bite.

The Ursidae are unique among the Carnivora, being the only family in which nearly all members have become principally vegetarian omnivores. Flesh is relatively easy to digest; carnivores therefore have very short guts and simple stomachs, in contrast to the long guts and complex, multi-chambered stomachs of ruminants (such as antelopes), which are needed in order to digest vegetation. Bears are not the only members of the order to have secondarily abandoned carnivory in favour of omnivory, the procyonid kinkajou (*Potos flavus*) specializes in nectar-feeding, the hyaenid aardwolf (*Proteles cristatus*) subsists on termites and the European badger (*Meles meles*) eats mostly earthworms. For such animals short guts and simple stomachs may have become a considerable handicap.

CLASSIFICATION

As arctoid fissipeds, bears have closer affinities to dogs than to cats. Of the eight living species of bears, six belong to the genus *Ursus*; they are closely related and thought to be of relatively recent evolutionary origin. The spectacled bear (*Tremarctos ornatus*) and giant panda (*Ailuropoda melanoleuca*) are the sole living representatives of much older lineages of the bear family.

In order to clarify the relationships which exist between living animal species, molecular scientists have devised a number of techniques based on the premise that the greater the length of evolutionary time which separates two species, the more different they will be in terms of the make-up of their genetic material, enzymes and major histocompatibility complexes. In simpler terms this means that species which share a recent, common ancestor will be more alike than those which diverged from the lineage further back in the past.

Clearly, results of such analyses assume greater certainty as an increasing number of different molecular structures are compared. It has often been found that, when only a few such structures are looked at, the conclusions tend to be equivocal.

In addition to indicating degree of relatedness between different species of animals, such techniques may also give an idea of how long ago in time individual species evolved. This sort of dating is based on the idea of a 'molecular clock', an evolutionary timescale calibrated on the assumption that differences in genetic material accumulate at a constant (and known) rate. Although based on sound theoretical principles, a number of valid

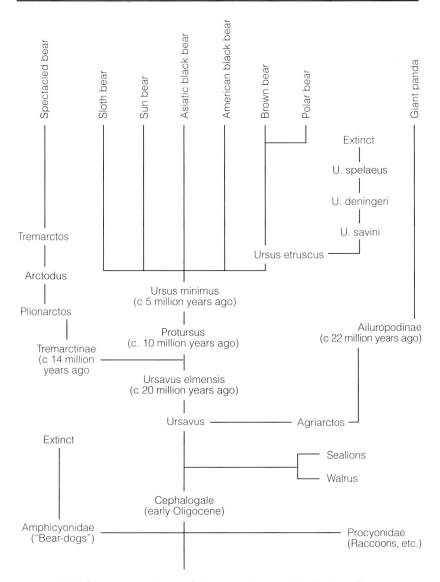

A brief evolutionary history of the extant bears and their close allies.

objections to this concept have been raised; it therefore becomes imposs-ible to view dates derived by these techniques as anything more than approximations. Nonetheless, it is again true that the greater the number of molecular structures looked at, the less important are the confounding events and so the datings assume a somewhat greater accuracy.

As controls for these techniques, it is usual to examine one or two species belonging to a separate, but still quite closely related group. These are the '*outgroup comparisons*' which should, when the final conclusions are drawn, be shown to be more distantly related to the '*ingroup species*'. Species used as outgroups are chosen on the basis of an understanding of the fossil history of the group concerned. It is extremely important to choose the outgroup carefully; to examine bear phylogeny using a mouse as the outgroup comparison is pointless as the considerable difference between the two is of little use in strengthening conclusions drawn from the analysis. Outgroup species should be closely related to the ingroup but not a part of it – dogs or raccoons would be appropriate outgroup choices in examining bear phylogeny.

In order to establish the relatedness between bears, pandas and raccoons, four independent molecular and genetic features have been analysed, involving chromosomes, enzymes, immunological molecules and the DNA itself. Using data derived from these molecules, and employing the dog as an outgroup comparison, a consensus phylogeny has been erected which shows procyonids and ursids to have diverged from one another between 70 million and 40 million years ago; very soon after this event the red panda diverged as an early member of the procyonid line. Other researchers, using similar methods, have placed the divergence of the ursid and procyonid lineages as much later than the original estimates – between 32 million and 23 million years ago; this is now felt to be a more accurate assessment of the actual date.

Among bears, the giant panda was the first modern species to arise (between 22 million and 18 million years ago), followed shortly by the spectacled bear (*Tremarctos ornatus*). The dog was found to lie consistently outside of the group under analysis, as expected.

The red panda (*Ailurus fulgens*), which is restricted to certain parts of Asia today, has several similarities to the giant panda and for some time these two animals were classified together. Today we recognize the red panda as a member of the Procyonidae.

The raccoon (*Procyon lotor*) of North America is the most widely known member of the Procyonidae.

On the basis of molecular structures, the spectacled bear is consistently found to be very different from the six species of the genus *Ursus*, having diverged from the pre-ursine line early (between 15 million and 10 million years ago). This agrees with expectations based on the fossil history of the family (see Chapter 3).

The remaining six species of living bear are members of the ursine branch of the family. They are: the American black bear (*Ursus americanus*), the brown bear (*U. arctos*), the polar bear (*U. maritimus*) and the three small Asian bears – sun bear (*U. malayanus*), sloth bear (*U. ursinus*) and Asiatic black bear (*U. thibetanus*). Apart from the polar bear, all members of the ursine line are roughly the same age, first appearing between 8 million and 4 million years ago; molecular data have not been able to identify unequivocally specific relationships within this ursine group. There is however, a strong suggestion that the polar bear is a very recent evolutionary modification of the brown bear, first appearing only 2–3 million years ago.

THE RIDDLE OF THE GIANT PANDA

Ursid phylogeny presents two problems in the form of the giant and red pandas. Both species were originally described for Western science at the end of the nineteenth century by the great naturalist and missionary, Père Armand David. He was the first to discover the red panda (*Ailurus fulgens*) and dispatched a report of its appearance and behaviour back to the West. London Zoo soon received a live specimen but, upon receipt, were dismayed to find that it bore little resemblance to the animal described by Père David. Rather than a beautiful, orange-red animal with a curious and amenable disposition, they found themselves in possession of a rather bad-tempered, listless and lacklustre beast. Furthermore, it refused all proffered food (which happened to be meat) and rapidly became dangerously weak.

43

More by accident than judgement it suddenly became clear that the red panda was actually a vegetarian and so, unsurprisingly, had not been tempted by the various meaty titbits previously offered. This was confusing to authorities of the period since morphological affinities clearly placed the red panda in the Carnivora. Nonetheless, once its diet had been recognized, it rapidly transformed into the animal that had originally been expected on the basis of early reports.

Next, Père David went in search of the elusive 'bamboo-bear' which, the Chinese informed him, roamed the forested hills and valleys of northern and western China. Upon finally locating it Père David had no trouble in identifying it as a bear. The same cannot be said for Western science which, on examination of various aspects of its skeleton and soft anatomy, initiated an argument which even today has not been fully settled to everybody's satisfaction.

The problem arose because the giant panda shares some features of its anatomy with the red panda; since the latter had already been classified as belonging to the raccoon family (Procyonidae) the giant panda was placed there also. At this time the name 'bamboo-bear' was dropped in favour of 'giant panda' as a reflection of its considered affinity; this name has stuck ever since.

In the succeeding controversy, all possible combinations of solution have, at one time or another, been offered – red and giant pandas both as bears or both as procyonids, as one or other and, in some instances, as neither but rather as specialists in a group all of their own. In neither case does the scant fossil record yield any helpful information. Molecular techniques have, however, produced their solution to this riddle – the giant panda is a bear, albeit a rather specialized and ancient one, and the red panda is a procyonid, the ancestors of which crossed the Bering land-bridge from North America into Eurasia during the Pliocene – there are now several specimens of the ancestral genus, *Parailurus*, from both continents. Although this has generally met with acceptance, there remains, in the minds of a few, some doubt.

It might be felt that the resemblance which the giant panda has to bears should have been sufficient to forestall any doubt regarding its taxonomic affinity. However, all participants in this debate had valid grounds for defending their stance. From the currently accepted viewpoint of it being a bear, it must be admitted that it has some very unbear-like characteristics which are worth discussing briefly.

There were never any doubts that the giant panda belonged to the Carnivora, despite the fact that it rarely eats meat, subsisting rather on a diet comprised almost entirely of bamboo. Recent field work has now shown that its diet is not so rigid as was originally believed (see Chapter 4) but still it is very specialized. Nonetheless, a principally vegetarian diet should not have created too great a stir as all bears, with the exception of the polar bear, have abandoned obligate carnivory in favour of a more plant-based diet.

Certain other characteristics of the giant panda are rather unbear-like though and strongly resemble the state found in red pandas. The enlarged shoulder and neck region and reduced hindquarters, responsible for the giant pandas' ambling gait, are adaptations allowing the large head and masticatory apparatus to be accommodated – both necessary in order to cope with the bamboo diet, as in the red panda.

More significant similarities with the procyonid red panda are found in two skeletal accessory structures. The first is the false thumb discussed above. The second is a stiffening rod (baculum) found in the soft tissue of the penis. Most carnivores possess such a structure, which functions to prolong copulation and induce ovulation in the female. Baculum structure is quite species-specific: in all bears it is straight and forwardly directed; in both red and giant pandas it is S-shaped and backwardly directed.

In addition to these features, pandas do not behave like typical bears; whereas most bears have a period of annual dormancy (see Chapter 5), pandas do not. Also, bears tend to roar or growl; pandas, on the other hand, rarely do so and are most often heard to produce a rather feeble bleat.

In view of these facts, it becomes clear why some zoologists were reluctant to place the giant panda among the bears. Although it is certainly true that structures may arise independently in different groups of animal (wings, for instance, are found in both birds and bats, but nobody seriously suggests that they be grouped together!), evolution may independently arrive at similar solutions; usually, however, there are significant differences in the details of such structures (the wings of birds and bats, for instance, are totally different). In the case of the giant and red pandas some of the structures (the baculum and radial sesamoid) are sufficiently similar to suggest that the possibility of their independent evolutionary origin is rather low; nonetheless, it is now generally believed that this is the case.

THE LIVING BEARS

Results of phylogenetic analyses show that the eight living species of bear belong to three subfamilies: Tremarctinae (spectacled bear), Ailuropodinae (giant panda) and Ursinae (all others). All bears have large heads and large, heavily built bodies with short, strong limbs and short tails. Eyes and ears are small, ears being erect and rounded. All have 5 digits on each limb and each digit is armed with a long, recurved and non-retractile claw. The gait is plantigrade and, among the predominantly terrestrial species, the soles of the feet are hairy; among more arboreal species the soles are naked. Apart from the spectacled bear (in which it is rather short), the snout is long and in all species the lips are free from the gums and protrusible.

The massive skull is immediately recognizable by the absence of an inflated tympanic bulla (see Chapter 3). All species have between 34 and 42 teeth; the dental formula is I (incisors) 3/3, C (canines) 1/1, P (premolars) 2–4/2–4, M (molars) 2/3; individual species show variation in the number of premolar teeth present. The sloth bear has only 40 teeth but one upper incisor on either side of the jaw has been lost; there is a full premolar complement in this species. In all cases the incisors are unspecialized and the canines are elongate; the anterior three premolars are very much reduced, while the molars are broad and flat, showing little evidence of carnassial specialization, reflecting the trend away from carnivory and a predatory life-style.

Bears rely principally on their sense of smell; eyesight and hearing are poor, making them easily startled in the field. A surprised bear is a

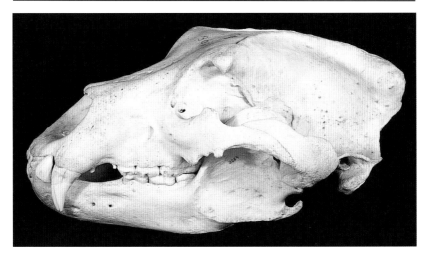

Skull of a male brown bear (*Ursus arctos*) showing the long snout, low cranium and large caninė teeth.

Skull of a sun bear (*Ursus malayanus*). This species has a much shorter and more compact head than the brown bear.

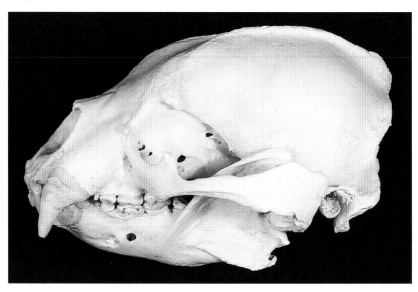

very dangerous animal; when hiking in places where bears may occur it is advisable to make as much noise as possible in order to avoid surprising a resting bear.

Most species of bear enter a period of winter dormancy, usually in a den prepared in a secure location. Although often referred to as 'hibernation', this is not strictly the case – hibernation involves a state of metabolic quiescence during which body temperature, respiratory rate and other metabolic

Although no longer actively predatory, bears still possess large canine teeth.

processes are reduced. In bears these features are believed generally not to pertain; bears can usually be readily roused from their sleep, unlike animals in true hibernation. Some research has, however, suggested that there are considerable physiological changes as well as a 50 per cent drop in heart rate during this period; the terms 'torpor' or 'semi-hibernation' therefore seem applicable (see Chapter 5).

Giant Panda (*Ailuropoda melanoleuca*)

This species is quite unmistakable with its thick, woolly white coat and black legs, ears, shoulders and eyes; in some individuals the black areas have a chestnut-red tinge. Although previously extensive, the current range of this species is restricted to Sichuan, Gansu and Shanxi Provinces of central China.

Giant pandas are one of the smallest of bears standing only 70–80cm (27½–31½in) at the shoulder and being only 1.6–1.9m (5¼–6¼ft) long from nose to rump. Males and females are only slightly different in size terms,

The giant panda (*Ailuropoda melanoleuca*) is the rarest of the bears. It is today restricted to small pockets in China where conservation measures are strictly enforced.

with males only 10–20 per cent heavier than females (male 85–125kg/ 187–276lb); female 70–100kg/154–220lb). Sexes are notoriously difficult to differentiate, even with quite detailed genital examination.

Litters tend to be small with usually only one or two cubs born. At birth, cubs weigh 85–140g (3–5oz) each. Occasionally, a female may give birth to three cubs but, in any event, it is rare for more than one cub of the litter to survive to adulthood.

The natural longevity of giant pandas is unknown; in captivity they may live for more than 20 years. Females have a single, brief oestrus each year, during which period they are most receptive for between only 1 and 5 days. Although mating takes place between March and May, litters are born from August and September onwards, implantation having been delayed by between 45 and 120 days.

Pandas have proven to be remarkably difficult to breed in captivity and reproductive success in the wild is probably also low. This, together

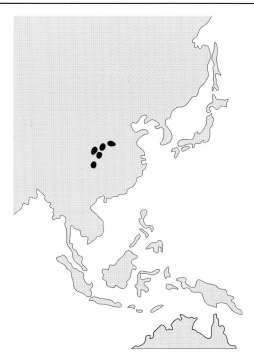

Distribution of the giant panda, *Ailuropoda melanoleuca.*

with problems of poaching, habitat loss and human encroachment, have conspired to make this bear extremely rare. Today it is the well-known symbol of the World Wide Fund for Nature (WWF) and is regarded in China as a national treasure, the killing of which carries the death penalty. The Chinese Government has initiated a considerable conservation effort and, together with George Schaller of the New York Zoological Society, has conducted extensive research into its ecology and behaviour.

Spectacled Bear (*Tremarctos ornatus*)

This is the only species of bear to be found in South America, where is is restricted to the mountainous regions of Peru, Ecuador, Colombia and Venezuela. Some reports have also suggested its presence in eastern Panama and northern Argentina. The rather shaggy coat is uniformly dark brown or black in colour, except for circular, light-coloured markings around the eyes and across the bridge of the short muzzle. These markings, to which the bear owes its name, are very variable and may extend down the throat and onto the chest in some individuals.

Measuring 1.5–1.8m (5–6ft) from nose to rump, standing 70–90cm (27½–35½in) at the shoulder and weighing 100–155kg (220–342lb), this is a moderately sized bear; females are some 30–40 per cent smaller than males.

Details of reproductive behaviour in the wild are sparse. Mating takes place from April to June and litters are born between November and

The spectacled bear (*Tremarctos ornatus*) is the only bear species found in South America today. Its name derives from the spectacle-like facial markings.

February. In captive animals pregnancy has been found to last for up to 8 months and seems to involve a period of delayed implantation. Between one and three cubs are born, each weighing 300–360g (10½–12½oz). The lifespan of wild spectacled bears is unknown; captive animals usually live to 20 or 25 years of age although a single animal at Buenos Aires Zoo reached an age of 36 years.

Persecution and habitat loss due to human encroachment have led to a decline in the range of this bear. In Peru it is hunted for its meat and fur, and population fragmentation, resulting in the isolation of individuals, has become a severe threat to their reproductive success.

Distribution of the spectacled bear, *Tremarctos ornatus*.

Sun Bear (*Ursus malayanus*)

The sun bear is the smallest of the bears, standing only 70cm (27½in) at the shoulder and measuring 1.2–1.5m (4–5ft) from nose to rump. Males are only 10–20 per cent heavier than females, weighing 27–65kg (15–143lb). The short coat is uniformly black, other than a light patch on the chest and a grey muzzle. The chest patch is very variable, being U-shaped in some individuals and all but absent in others.

The natural range of this species, although not fully researched, is probably greater than its currently known range – the densely forested areas of Peninsular Malaysia, Borneo, Sumatra, Burma, Thailand and Indo-China. It is also reported to be present in small, isolated pockets in the southern Yunnan Province of China although there have been no recent sightings.

Very little is known about the reproductive biology of this species; in the wild it seems that cubs may be born at any time of year. In captive animals, gestation periods have been found to range from 95 to 240 days and, as with other bears, this is the result of delayed implantation and gives little

The sun bear (*Ursus malayanus*) is the smallest of the living bears. Very little is known about this species although it is, mistakenly, considered to be a good pet in certain parts of Asia.

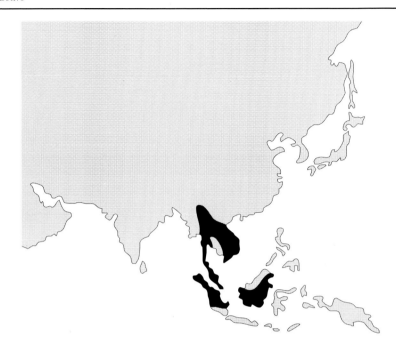

Distribution of the sun bear, *Ursus malayanus.*

idea as to the females most receptive periods. Litters contain one or two young, each weighing 325g (11½oz).

In some places sun bears are considered good pets but they often become uncontrollable after 3 or 4 years and are then either abandoned or killed. In the wild this bear is often cited as one of the most dangerous animals of its range. Habitat destruction seems to be having an adverse effect on population numbers.

Sloth Bear (*Ursus ursinus*)

Sloth bears are small and black, sporting a long, shaggy coat; the presence of brown and grey hairs in the coat may give the appearance of a tawny or cinnamon colouration. The face around the eyes and the muzzle are grey and there is a light U- or Y-shaped patch on the chest. Adults measure 1.5–1.9m (5–6¼ft) in length and stand 60–90cm (23½–35½in) at the shoulder. Males are 30–40 per cent heavier than females, weighing 80–140kg (176–309lb).

Mating takes place between May and July, although peak receptivity of females is probably very brief. Pregnancy lasts 6–7 months and results in litters of one or two cubs, occasionally three.

Sloth bears are distributed throughout India and Sri Lanka; they also probably extend further north into Bangladesh, Nepal and Bhutan. In the past this bear has been extensively hunted due to its reputation for aggression and crop destruction. Today it is suffering through habitat loss due to a number of agricultural and developmental schemes.

The sloth bear (*Ursus ursinus*) is instantly recognizable by its thick, shaggy coat.

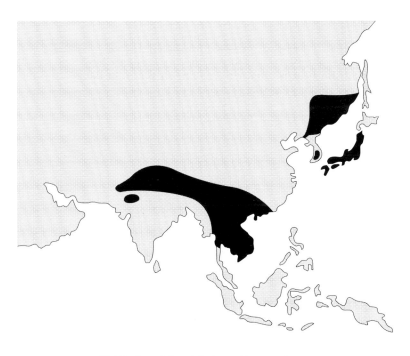

Distribution of the sloth bear, *Ursus ursinus.*

Asiatic Black Bear (*Ursus thibetanus*)

This bear is medium-sized and usually uniformly black, except for its light-coloured muzzle and a distinctive white chevron extending out to the shoulders from the chest. In some areas, individuals may appear to have a more brown coloration. The ears appear large in proportion to the rest of the head.

This species is distributed over a considerable area of South-East and eastern Asia, being found in mountainous regions from Afghanistan, Pakistan and northern India, through Nepal, Sikkim and Bhutan, and into China, Thailand, Laos, Kampuchea and Vietnam. Isolated populations also occur on Taiwan and the Japanese islands of Honshu and Shikoku. In the

The Asiatic black bear (*Ursus thibetanus*), like the sloth bear, has a shaggy coat but, unlike the sloth bear, has a distinctive white chevron extending across its chest.

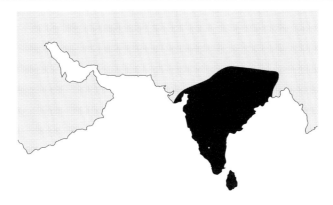

Distribution of the Asiatic black bear, *Ursus thibetanus*.

early twentieth century zoologists recognized four subspecies: *U. t. japonicus* (Japan), *U. t. formosanus* (Taiwan), *U. t. ussuricus* (Mongolia) and *U. t. thibetanus* (all other regions). Today these are considered only to be racial variants; a single true subspecies is recognized – *U. t. gedrosianus*, of southern Pakistan.

Adults measure 1.3–1.9m (4¼–6¼ ft) in length. Adult males weigh 100–200kg (220–440lb), up to twice the size of adult females (50–125kg/110–275lb). Life spans of wild bears average approximately 24 years.

In more northern populations, mating is reported to take place in June and July; in more southerly areas of its range mating occurs later, in October. The gestation period is unclear and, as with other bears, almost certainly involves a period of delayed implantation. Usually a pair of cubs are born.

The Asiatic black bear is suffering from the encroachment of human activities into its habitat.

American Black Bear (*Ursus americanus*)

This medium-sized bear measures 1.3–1.9m (4¼–6¼ft) in length and stands 80–95cm (31½–37¼in) at the shoulder. Adult males, weighing 60–300kg (132–661lb), are 20–60 per cent heavier than females. Most individuals are a uniform black colour with a lighter muzzle. However, not all of these bears are black; indeed there is considerable variation of colour. Brown and reddish-brown individuals are quite common and blue-black and white bears of this species also exist but are rare.

Early settlers and pioneers of North America became understandably confused by the extreme colour variability of this bear and up to 18 subspecies have been described on the basis of differences in size, distribution and colour; some of these may not be true subspecies but, merely racial variants. The Kermode bear (*U. a. kermodei*) of Gribble Island and neighbouring coastal areas of British Columbia may be pure white; this is a distinct colour phase, accounting for some 10 per cent of bears in this area, and not merely albinism. In adjacent areas, recognized subspecies are the blue, or glacier, bear (*U. a. emmansii*), of northern British Columbia and the Yukon,

American black bears (*Ursus americanus*) show considerable habitat adaptability, extending from the cold north to the warmer south.

Distribution of the American black bear, *Ursus americanus.*

U. a. altifrontalis of southwestern British Colombia, the large *U. a. carlottae* from the Queen Charlotte Islands and *U. a. vancouveri* of Vancouver Island. In addition to these are the cinnamon bear (*U. a. cinnamomum*) of southwestern Canada and western USA, the Newfoundland bear (*U. a. hamiltoni*), the Floridan bear (*U. a. floridanus*) and the east Texan bear (*U. a. luteolus*). This last subspecies once ranged from Texas into Mississippi but today is considered very rare and possibly even extinct. The status of these subspecies, particularly mainland ones, is highly debatable.

This species clearly has a considerable distribution across North America where it is generally not thought to be endangered or vulnerable, although specific populations may be.

As might be expected, there is a considerable body of information regarding the biology and ecology of this species. Animals may live for up to 32 years in the wild, males and females leading essentially solitary lives, coming together only for the purposes of mating in June and July. Females usually give birth every other year but may, for a number of possible reasons, delay breeding for 3 or 4 years. Including a period of delayed implantation, pregnancy lasts about 220 days and results in litters of usually two or three, cubs, although up to five have been reported. Cubs weigh 225–330g (8–11½oz) at birth.

Above: American black bears are often confused with brown bears since they may often have a similar coloration; both animals in this picture are black bears.

The colour variation of American black bears is extreme, ranging from white to black through various shades of intermediate colours. This red coloration is quite common in certain areas.

Brown Bear (*Ursus arctos*)

Although not generally accepted as the largest of the bears, an honour which goes to the polar bear, the brown bear comes a very close second, adult males weighing in at 135–390kg (298–860lb); adult females are smaller 95–205kg (209–452lb). Lengths of 2.8m (9¼ft) and shoulder heights of 1.5m (5ft) are common. Nonetheless, Kodiak brown bears have been recorded which have proportions more in the polar bear range.

Brown bears have the widest natural distribution of any bear species, being found in localized pockets throughout western Europe, the Middle East, eastern Europe, across northern Eurasia to Japan and into Alaska and western Canada. Within the USA they are found in isolated pockets in the states of Washington, Idaho, Montana and Wyoming. Where ranges of brown bears overlap with those of brown-colour-phase black bears, confusion may occur over identification. This is further complicated by the fact that brown bears, usually a dark brown colour, may also be any shade between light cream and black. Size differences between the two species are some assistance in recognition but, more importantly, brown bears have a characteristic hump over the shoulders and a markedly concave face. Brown bears tend to be more aggressive than black bears (although aggression is usually a response to being startled) and, unlike American black bears, do not climb trees.

As with American black bears, brown bears have been the subject of considerable taxonomic 'splitting' into subspecies, the 'grizzly' (*U. a. horribilis*) is probably the best known and the term refers to the grizzled coloration, an effect produced by the tip of the hairs being lighter in colour than the shank. Although often used to describe brown bears generally, it is more usually confined to American populations. Eurasian brown bears are recognized as a separate subspecies – *U. a. arctos*.

Eight other subspecies have also been described: the Kodiak bear (*U. a. middendorffi*) of Kodiak, Afognak and Shuyak Islands, the Siberian bear (*U. a. beringianus*), the red bear (*U. a. isabellinus*) of northern India and the Himalayas, the Manchurian bear (*U. a. manchuricus*), the horse bear

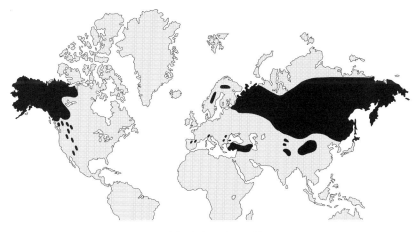

Distribution of the brown bear, *Ursus arctos*.

Brown bears (*Ursus arctos*) have a wide natural distribution throughout the northern hemisphere. This American bear is also known as the 'grizzly' bear by virtue of the grizzled colour of the coat.

Brown bears, like black bears, come in different colours. This red (cinnamon bear) form is from Asia.

(*U. a. pruinosus*) of Tibet, Sichuan and western China, the Hokkaido bear (*U. a. yesoensis*) of Japan, the Bajan bear (*U. a. californicus*) of California and Baja, and the Mexican bear (*U. a. nelsoni*). The Bajan bear is known to have become extinct in the 1920s; the Siberian brown bear may be the animal referred to in accounts of the legendary, gigantic brown bears which roam the wastes of Kamchatka.

In the wild, brown bears may live for 25–30 years. Mating takes place between May and June; implantation is delayed until October or November and between one and four cubs are born from January to March. Cubs weigh, at birth, 340–680g (12–24oz).

Polar Bear (*Ursus maritimus*)

Weighing up to 600kg (1,323lb) exceptionally up to 800kg (1,764lb) – and measuring 2.6m (8½ft) at the shoulder – an adult male polar bear is the largest of bears. Females are considerably smaller than males, weighing up to 300kg (661lb). They are immediately recognizable with their creamy-white coat and relatively long neck. The nose, lips and soles of the feet are black as, indeed, is the skin beneath the coat.

Polar bears have a circumpolar, Arctic distribution extending as far south as James Bay in Canada (which lies at more or less the same latitude as London, UK). As the pack ice advances, polar bears move into New-foundland and the northern Bering Sea, returning north as the ice recedes. No current subspecies are recognized, although in 1964 the fossil remains of a large form, *U. m. tyrannicus*, was excavated in southern England.

Unlike all other bears, polar bears are primarily carnivorous, existing mostly on ringed seals and, to some extent, bearded seals. In addition they have been reported to prey on young walrus and be able to catch beluga and narwhal as they come close to the shore. Their diet is supplemented with grass, berries and kelp.

Mating takes place between the ends of March and May, implantation is delayed until September or October and a litter of one to four cubs, each weighing 600–700g (21–24¾oz) is produced between November and January. Most litters are of twins; four cubs is probably an extreme rarity.

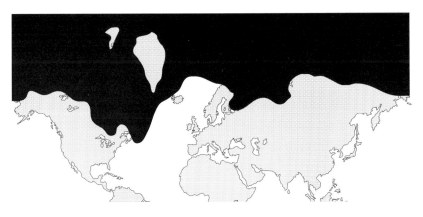

Distribution of the polar bear, *Ursus maritimus.*

The polar bear *(Ursus maritimus)* is the largest of the bears and also the most recently evolved, having diverged from a brown-bear ancestor only about 3 million years ago.

The predatory lifestyle of this species demands an extended period of parental care by the female. For this reason females tend to be able to mate only once every 3–4 years. The life span of wild polar bears is up to 25 years.

Despite its large size and general preference for inhospitable habitats, this bear has not escaped human attention. Native peoples have long hunted them for their fur, fat and meat. This was aggravated in the early twentieth century when bears became the object of increased hunting pressure from trophy-hunters. Several countries have now prohibited hunting of polar bears, other than by native peoples, by acts of law. Increased interest in this bear led to an international agreement for habitat protection and research in 1976.

Chapter 3
Evolution of Bears

ORIGINS OF THE CARNIVORA

With the final demise of dinosaurs, some 65 million years ago, many predatory life-style niches became available for new occupants. One type of animal which vied for these positions were small, arboreal mammals, members of the family Miacidae. Mammals were not a new group of animal; they had existed alongside the dinosaurs as inconspicuous, tree-dwelling and probably mainly nocturnal animals for millions of years. Whatever caused the extinction of the highly successful reptilian groups left the mammals all but untouched; it did, however, open up a multitude of opportunities for them. Over the intervening period of time, the miacids gave rise to the highly successful and diverse group of animals that is today called the Carnivora. Some members of this group came to specialize in tactical predatory behaviour, while others remained more generalist, preying upon other animals where possible but supplementing their diet with vegetation, insects and fruit. One family all but abandoned their predatory history, reverting to an essentially vegetarian life-style – the bears.

The appearance of the Miacidae was almost immediately (in geological terms) accompanied, some 60 million years ago, by the group splitting into two, giving on one hand the cat branch (aeluroid or viverravines) and on the other, the dog (arctoid or vulpavine) branch. At this time, however, these animals did not have sole claim to the predatory niche: in the northern hemisphere the Condylarthra (distant ancestors of whales and ungulates) and the Creodonta also pursued this way of life; in the southern hemisphere, the phororhacoids ('thunder birds') and carnivorous marsupials held sway. The last of the condylarths became extinct 34 million years ago; the creodonts followed them into oblivion more recently, about 8 million years ago. In the northern hemisphere the Carnivora finally assumed dominance among predators between 30 million and 20 million years ago.

On the southern continents, marsupials had diversified and successfully filled all the ecological niches which newer, eutherian (placental) mammals were occupying on the northern land-masses. The marsupials had themselves originated in what is now North America at a time when all land formed a single, equatorial band; as this land-mass broke apart, some blocks moving north and others south, the eutherians evolved in the northern areas. Marsupials thrived in isolation on the southern continents until the continental land-masses shifted toward their current orientation. Marsupials living on what is now Antarctica died out while those living on the South American land-mass came into contact with their eutherian counterparts as the Panamanian land-bridge opened some 2 million years ago. Only a few marsupial species survived the influx of placental mammals into South America; Australia, isolated and therefore immune to invasion, became the only secure haven for these mammals.

In the northern hemisphere, drifting of continental land-masses created periodic connections between areas which are now separated by water. One important such connection was the land-bridge between eastern Asia and western North America across the Bering Straits, connecting what are now Siberia and Alaska; this provided a means by which animals could re-distribute themselves between the Old and New Worlds. Vulpavine miacids, primarily of the New World, crossed into the Old World and, conversely, the originally Old World viverravines crossed into the Americas.

From these small arboreal hunters evolved the full range of today's Carnivora. From the viverravines arose the dedicated, predatory cats (Felidae), powerful and opportunistic hyaenas (Hyaenidae), nimble and inconspicuous genets and civets (Viverridae) and the slender, and some-times social, mongooses (Herpestidae). The vulpavine (or dog) branch of the Miacidae gave rise to the strong, coursing dogs (Canidae), the generalist and opportunistic raccoons (Procyonidae), the small, deadly and somewhat odorous stoats, weasels, badgers, otters and skunks (Mustelidae) and the large, essentially vegetarian bears (Ursidae).

In addition to these groups, all of which have representatives alive today, the vulpavine branch also gave rise to two other groups which, over the course of time have both become extinct. The paleosabres were early cat-like forms with exaggerated canines (arising from within the Canidae) which finally became extinct 6 million years ago; this style of animal also evolved, independently, among the Felidae. The Amphicyonidae (or bear-dogs), the second of these groups, passed into extinction some 8 million years ago; although closely related to bears they also showed many features characteristic of dogs.

FIRST BEARS

The bear chapter of the carnivore evolutionary story started 34 million years ago with an agile, tree-top hunter, about the size of a fox, called *Cephalogale*, which hunted through the forests of Asia. It is only recently that this animal has been recognized as a bear; because of its resemblance to early canids it was included with that family for many years. In the trees of the primitive Asian forests, *Cephalogale* was a dedicated carnivore, possessing a full set of premolar teeth and the all-important carnassial teeth (which had evolved some 30 million years earlier in the Miacidae). The dentition characteristic of bears was to appear at a later date.

Unfortunately, the trail of the bear story is lost some 15 million years after the appearance of *Cephalogale*. Although it has been possible to reconstruct some of the events of this period there is little in the way of direct fossil evidence to support such ideas. One reason for this hiatus is the fact that these animals were evolving in forest habitats; fossilization is an unlikely event under the best possible circumstances and, in forests, the chances of such events occurring become almost non-existent.

It is known that, during this period (between 30 million and 27 million years ago), the sea-lions (Otariidae) and walrus (Odobenidae) appeared

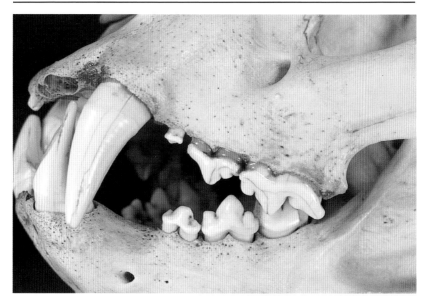

In dedicated carnivores, such as this tiger (*Panthera tigris*), the carnassial teeth are well developed. The blade-like extensions of both the last upper premolar and first lower molar can clearly be seen in this photograph.

and that they evolved from the bear lineage (as demonstrated by morphological, dental, and molecular similarities). The development of these animals from an early bear, existing in coastal habitats and hunting primarily in water, is not too difficult to visualize; today's polar bear leads a somewhat similar life-style to that hypothesized for the putative ancestor of these two pinniped families. At about the same time a similar set of events took place and gave rise to the true seals (Phocidae) from an ancestor within the mustelid lineage; the transitional animal may have had a life-style like that of today's sea otter (*Enhydra lutris*).

A little over 20 million years ago, the threads of the bear story can be once again found in the form of the terrier-sized *Ursavus elmensis*, the 'Dawn Bear'. Little had occurred to advance the bears to their present condition during the 15 million years separating *Cephalogale* from *U. elmensis*; this 'dawn bear' was still small and probably still conducted much of its hunting in the tree-tops. Importantly, it still retained a full set of premolars and carnassial teeth. However, these carnassials had become reduced in size and the posterior molar teeth had now developed expanded chewing and grinding surfaces; *Ursavus* was now clearly supplementing its diet with plant and insect material.

The genus *Ursavus* is pivotal to the story of bears as it is ancestral to all of the living species in this family. Taxonomists place it, together with two other genera also alive at that time – *Indarctos* and *Agriotherium* – in the subfamily Agriotheriinae. Although all members of this subfamily had become extinct by the end of the Pliocene (2.5 million years ago), the three living subfamilies (Ursinae, Tremarctinae and Ailuropodinae) are believed to have derived from later members of the genus *Ursavus*.

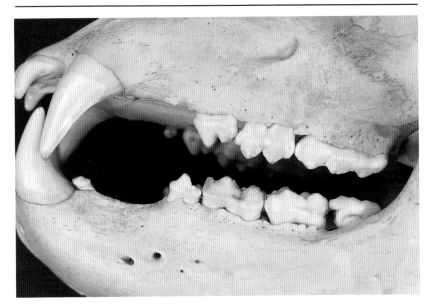

Bears have mostly abandoned the predatory way of life and have, over the course of evolutionary time, lost the carnassial blades; this can be seen by comparing this photograph of the cheek teeth of a brown bear with that of the tiger.

The Ailuropodinae, of which the giant panda (*Ailuropoda melanoleuca*) is the single living representative, evolved within the bear family between 25 million and 18 million years ago, although the genus *Ailuropoda* appears, without fossil precursor, during the Early Pleistocene, some 3 million years ago. However, the earliest member of the subfamily is thought to have been *Agriarctos*, a poorly known genus which appeared in the Early Miocene, some 20 million years ago.

During the Pleistocene, pandas were considerably more widely distributed than they are today; it has previously been believed that the genus comprised four species, a more recent re-evaluation of the material suggests that there were, in fact, only two – *Ailuropoda microta* and *A. melanoleuca*. The former of these was about half the size of the modern-day giant panda and lived in South-East Asia during the Early Pleistocene; the giant panda of today (*A. melanoleuca*) first appears in the Mid-Pleistocene. Fossils of pandas have been recovered (with a single exception in Thailand) only from China, their distribution having extended from Beijing in the north to the coastal areas of the south and east and as far west as Thailand. Mid- and Late Pleistocene sites are much more common than sites yielding older (Early Pleistocene) fossils; these tend to be restricted to the south of China. The fossil sites also tend to be mostly confined to hill and plateau areas surrounding the Huang He and Chang Jiang (Yellow and Yangtze) Rivers; this almost certainly reflects the poor chance of fossilization on alluvial plains rather than the true distribution of the animals. Panda fossils are often found in association with fossils of the extinct elephant, *Stegodon*; so frequently is this species combination found that it is used to define a particular faunal assemblage.

The former distribution of giant pandas has been reduced to six small

Giant pandas are the only surviving members of the earliest group of bears to evolve.

areas on the eastern edge of the Tibetan plateau. Climatic variations during Pleistocene glacial and interglacial periods affected all of Eurasia and were, in some cases, quite extreme; there is little doubt that such climatic oscillations were, at least partly, indirectly responsible for the early decline in the pandas' range. The dentition of the earliest fossils strongly suggest that the species had specialized its diet to bamboo by the beginning of the Pleistocene. Although some species of bamboo are able to survive in areas where snow covers the ground for some part of the year, no species is able to tolerate the extreme and persistent periods of cold which would have existed during times of glacial advance. Such climatic variations would have proven difficult for bamboo and probably also rendered some areas suitable for alternative floral assemblages, thus forcing giant pandas to follow their staple food into smaller and smaller refugia.

Such climatic factors were compounded during the post-glacial Holocene by human activities. Dramatic reductions in the numbers of giant pandas and their exclusion from areas of their former range have been well documented since the middle of the eighteenth century. Expansion of human agriculture and development of townships have taken their toll. Unfortunately, this has been compounded by hunting pressure; recently panda pelts have been valued as sleeping mats, not only for their comfort value but also because, like many other animal-derived objects, they are believed to possess supernatural qualities, e.g. deterring the presence of ghosts and helping depict the future in dreams.

THE TREMARCTINE BEARS

The second subfamily to evolve from the Agriotheriinae was the Tremarctinae. Although today only a single representative remains, in the past this subfamily was both diverse and successful. Tremarctine bears probably evolved during the Miocene (some 15–12 million years ago), although the earliest fossil remains which can be definitely attributed to this group are much younger; the genus *Plionarctos* first appeared during the Upper Pliocene (*c.*5 million years ago). Both ursine and tremarctine bears originally evolved in the Eurasian forests where *Ursavus* roamed. The former subfamily remained in Eurasia for a considerable time, only crossing the Bering land-bridge to colonize the New World 8–7 million years ago. The tremarctine line, on the other hand, crossed into the Americas and diversified much earlier.

Although evolving early, tremarctines were slow to reach their potential in a land dominated by forests. The onset of considerable climatic change between 12 million and 10 million years ago started to thin the forests of the northern hemisphere, replacing them with expanses of open grassland. Within these novel habitats, new types of herbivore appeared to take advantage of these seas of grass and, with them, new forms of predator also evolved. In this new range dominated by open plains, tremarctine bears developed long legs and increased stamina for long chases, enabling them successfully to hunt deer.

The tremarctine bears reached the height of their success in North America during the Pleistocene (2–1.8 million years ago), at which time they were also able to take advantage of the newly formed Panamanian land-bridge and cross into South America, where today the sole remaining member of the subfamily exists – the spectacled bear (*Tremarctos ornatus*).

Three genera of tremarctine bear have been recognized: the first, *Plionarctos*, appeared during the Pliocene and was most probably ancestral to the other two – *Tremarctos* and *Arctodus* – both of which make their first appearance in the Pleistocene faunas of North and South America. Although the Pliocene threads of the tremarctine story are poorly known, fossils from Pleistocene deposits are both abundant and wide ranging.

The genus *Arctodus* has a quite complicated taxonomic history and although several North American species have been described they probably represent only two types.

The first group comprises relatively lightly built animals with small teeth, slender limbs and comparatively long faces. Members of the second group have shorter faces, larger cheek teeth and deeper, heavier lower jaws; limb bone dimensions suggest that these were larger and more powerfully built than members of the first group.

It is likely that these two groups reflect the fact that there were only two species of *Arctodus* present in North America: the lesser short-faced bear (*A. pristinus*) being the smaller, more slender, eastern arctodont of the first group, and the giant short-faced bear (*A. simus*) being the larger, heavier animal of the second group.

The lesser short-faced bear (*A. pristinus*) is known from only a few North American fossil localities, appearing in Irvingtonian (1.9–0.4 million years ago) deposits from Florida, West Virginia and Pennsylvania, and Rancholabrean (0.4–0.08 million years ago) deposits of Florida, South Carolina

Bears probably evolved in forested habitats similar to this in South America.

and West Virginia. The known history of this species seems to extend from 0.8–0.2 million years ago, the more recent period of which seems to have seen this species existing only as a relict in Florida. It was a quite primitive species of *Arctodus*; its face was only moderately shortened and its teeth were smaller and narrower than those of the larger *A. simus*. In terms of its way of life *A. pristinus* was probably less specialized than its larger relative. It is possible that the lesser short-faced bear represents a species which lies close to the origin of this genus and which was always confined to the eastern USA.

The giant short-faced bear (*A. simus*), on the other hand, was a widespread species with a long evolutionary history (*c.*2.4–0.08 million years ago). It can be distinguished from its smaller cousin not only by its larger size (the average size of a male was about 600kg/1,300lb although one specimen is estimated to have weighed 1,000kg/2,200lb when alive), but also by its bigger, broader and more crowded cheek teeth, shorter face and relatively longer limbs. Older, Irvingtonian fossils have been recovered from sites in Texas, California and Kansas; younger specimens, however, are distributed over a considerable range extending from Pennsylvania to California and from Alaska to Texas. Curiously, no specimens of this species have ever been recovered from Florida, a state rich in the fossils of several other bear species.

The long-legged, short-bodied build of these two species suggest that they were probably fast runners. In addition, their toes are directed forwards rather than slightly inwards, as is the case in other bears; this also suggests fast running ability with the claws acting in the fashion of 'spiked' running shoes. These features, together with other aspects of their skeletal and dental morphology, suggest arctodine bears led a highly predacious way of life, one which was more advanced in giant short-faced bears than their smaller cousins. High-domed skulls with prominent sagittal crests and the presence of a premassenteric fossa on the lower jaw are all adaptations for strong biting muscles, important not only for shearing off lumps of meat from carcasses but also in the delivery of the killing bite. As with their ancestor, *Ursavus*, short-faced bears retained the shearing blades on the carnassial teeth; the rather cat-like shortening of the face served to bring these teeth closer to the angle of the jaw where the full force of the strong musculature could be brought to best effect.

Although the ancestry of the giant short-faced bear is unknown, it is possible that it may have descended directly from the smaller *A. pristinus*, the general size of which changes over time, with individuals becoming larger as the species became progressively older. In the Yukon and Alaska, however, gigantic size persisted in this species until the Mid-Pleistocene (0.2 million years ago).

Although surviving into the Mid-Pleistocene, these short-faced bears finally passed into extinction. It is hard to know why this occurred; climatic change is an unlikely cause since individuals of the species survived equally well in the frozen wastes of the north and the burning heat of the south. It is equally unlikely that a decline in available prey was responsible since there is no indication that such an event took place. The most likely scenario is that increasing competition, from other predators for prey and from invading brown bears (*Ursus arctos*) for living space, coupled with changing vegetation patterns, exacerbated their demise. In several locations, remains of giant short-faced bears have been found alongside human artefacts suggesting that this species co-existed with Paleo-Indians prior to its extinction.

In addition to these two North American species of *Arctodus*, there are a further three species known from South America: *A. bonariensis* from La Plata and Buenos Aires (Brazil), *A. pamparus* from Argentina and *A. brasiliensis* from Brazil. As with their North American cousins, these species also probably led a predatory life-style. Although all members of the genus *Arctodus* are now extinct, in Pleistocene North America giant short-faced bears were probably the most powerful predators of their time.

The second genus of the subfamily Tremarctinae, *Tremarctos* itself, is less well known; only two species have been recovered – the extant spectacled bear (*T. ornatus*) and the North American spectacled bear or Floridan cave bear (*T. floridanus*). This genus appears to have evolved earlier than *Arctodus*, being found in Late Blancan deposits (*c*.2 million years ago) of Florida, New Mexico and Mexico, where remains are numerous; some evidence suggests that *Tremarctos* may have been present in even earlier times (*c*.2.3 million years ago). By the Early Rancholabrean (*c*.0.4 million years ago) this genus had extended its range north into Tennessee and Georgia; however, by Late Pleistocene times (*c*.0.2 million years ago) its range had receded and it was found only in the southern states. In Florida there is some evidence that this species may have survived into the Late Holocene; skeletal remains from the 'Devil's Den' sinkhole may be only 8,000 years old.

As with *Arctodus*, *Tremarctos* species are relatively small-toothed bears, usually retaining the full complement of premolars and possessing the mandibular premassenteric fossa indicative of a strong jaw musculature.

The ancestry of this genus is unclear; it probably derives from the poorly known Hemphilian (*c.*4 million years ago) genus, *Plionarctos*. However, unlike species of *Arctodus*, *Tremarctos* seems to have been primarily herbivorous, as is the spectacled bear of South America today.

In comparison with *T. ornatus*, *T. floridanus* was much larger and heavier, showing tendencies toward reduction of the anterior premolars and elongation of the posterior molars. Its head possessed a high-domed forehead and was carried on a relatively long neck; the body was barrel-like and the limbs were long and heavy. In terms of its morphology, the Floridan cave bear shows incipient features of the genus *Arctodus* as well as its sister species, *T. ornatus*. There is, however, no concrete evidence linking any of these species by direct descent from one another. The size increase of *T. floridanus* was probably driven by its vegetarian life-style and the need to protect itself. It is often found associated with remains of short-faced bears and also American black bears (*Ursus americanus*), although fossils of these latter two species are more often associated in open sites rather than in the caves preferred by the Floridan cave bear.

Of particular interest regarding *T. floridanus* is the remarkable resemblance it had to the European cave bears (*Ursus speleaus*), also a large, herbivorous bear with similar physical characteristics, the remains of which

The spectacled bear is the only tremarctine bear alive today. In the past these bears have been both highly successful and diverse.

are mostly found in cave sites. It has been proposed that such features in European cave bears were special adaptations to glacial conditions. For Floridan cave bears this cannot be the case since this species inhabited the lush, subtropical Gulf Coast states where the effects of higher latitude ice-sheet advances were not felt. This suggests that, in Europe, glacial conditions may have played only a subsidiary role in driving the evolution of the cave-bear physique.

Although smaller than its extinct cousin, *T. ornatus* shares many of its characteristics, e.g. the short face and dental arrangement. In other respects it is quite different: the limbs are relatively short and there is no excessive barrelling of the body. The spectacled bear is also a frequent tree-climber and thus clearly different in terms of its ecology. Little is known about its origin, but either this species or an immediate precursor form must have originated in North America, crossing to South America with the opening of the Panamanian land-bridge some 2 million years ago.

THE URSINE BEARS

Throughout the Miocene, the ursavine bears had been gradually increasing in size, with their dentition becoming more bear-like with the appearance of the characteristic broadened and flattened molars. During their time, ursavine bears were witness to large-scale changes in the habitats and faunas of the world. Some 18 million years ago, mastodons started to leave Africa, migrating into Eurasia and thence, via the Bering land-bridge, into the New World. Then 12 million years ago, moving in the opposite direction, *Hipparion*, the last of the three-toed horses, left North America for Asia, where it persisted for 10 million years until the new, one-toed horses followed it out of the New World.

The early *Hipparion* faunas of the Old World co-existed for some time with the last (and largest) of the ursavine bears. However, by this time *Ursavus* had given rise to another, more advanced type of bear – *Protursus* – the progenitor of the ursine lineage of bears.

The genus *Protursus* is known from very scant fossil material; indeed its original description was based on a single molar tooth found at a site near Barcelona in Spain. Nonetheless, paleontologists were able to show that this new species of bear, about the size of a large wolf, was a considerable advance on its ancestral, and contemporary, ursavines.

Some 12–10 million years ago the climate of the northern hemisphere started to become considerably drier, lush forests giving way to the more open bush and desert habitats preferred by antelope which, at this time, had entered a phase of dramatic evolutionary diversification. Bears, as typically forest inhabitants, fared less well during this period, *Ursavus* finally becoming extinct 8–7 million years ago.

It was not long before *Protursus* followed *Ursavus* into extinction (some even suggest that *Ursavus* may have outlived *Protursus*) but not before leaving a legacy in the form of *Ursus minimus* – the earliest of the recognizably true bears. Known from Pliocene (6–5 million years ago) fossil localities in southern France and Hungary, *U. minimus* is the most primitive species of the genus. Still small (about the size of the modern sun bear), it nonetheless shows some enlargement of its molar teeth, a trend to be continued in later species of *Ursus*. However, it still retained a full premolar complement and relatively long, slender canines.

At this time (6–5 million years ago) Eurasia was on the verge of a new ice age; the subtropical forests of the ursavines had already been replaced by more open habitats, with ursine bears occupying the newer, temperate forests. As the ice age drew closer, accelerated floral and faunal changes took place; elephants, following the earlier mastodons, left Africa for Eurasia where early, grazing bovine antelopes were already present. By 4 million years ago, *U. minimus*, albeit in a slightly modified form, was still present in Eurasia and, either this species or one very similar to it, was also to be found in North America.

Some researchers have suggested that *U. minimus* was the ancestor of both North American (*Ursus americanus*) and Asiatic (*Ursus thibetanus*) black bears; others favour the Etruscan bear (*Ursus etruscus*), a direct descendant of *U. minimus*, as their ancestor. The early presence of a smaller species of black bear in North America, *Ursus abstrusus*, suggests that the former is more likely. This species, also known as the 'primitive black bear', is poorly known and dates from the Blancan (*c*.2 million years ago); it was probably conspecific with *U. minimus* of Europe during the Ruscinian and Villafranchian (4–2 million years ago), suggesting a circumpolar, Holarctic population of black bears from which arose both North American and Asiatic extant species. In Eurasia, *Ursus mediterraneus*, from Mid-Pleistocene caves in Palestine, is probably an early form of *U. thibetanus*; some even believe it to be either a subspecies or a very close ally of the Asiatic black bear.

The Etruscan bear (*U. etruscus*) was typical of bears of this period of alternately cold glacial and warmer interglacial climates in Europe and Asia. Having already increased in size, it would become larger still before its disappearance some 1.5 million years ago, by which time it had achieved the size of a European brown bear. Although Etruscan bears still possessed a full set of premolar teeth they were considerably smaller than those of previous species. It is clear that the Etruscan bear gave rise to the brown bear (*U. arctos*) some 0.5 million years ago. Larger with longer, more slender limbs, *U. arctos* had also further reduced its premolar tooth sizes.

The earliest fossils of brown bears are found in China; it seems that Western populations of *U. etruscus* gave rise to cave bears whereas more eastern populations gave rise to brown bears. From this focus in the Orient they were ideally placed for migration both into North America and Europe, giving them, today, one of the widest natural distributions of any mammal. The first American indications for the presence of *U. arctos* are from Wisconsin (*c*.0.2 million years ago) deposits in Alaska, where they were conspecific with *Arctodus simus*.

The most recent bear to have evolved is the polar bear (*Ursus maritimus*) which has clearly derived from a population of brown bears. Adapted for a much more predatory life-style than other bears, polar bears specialize in hunting seals. Although fossils are very rare, some fragmentary remains are known from lava cave sites on the Pribiloff Islands; their date is uncertain but are most likely very recent. The earliest form of this species (*U. m. tyrannicus*) is only 100,000 years old and was excavated at a site near London, UK.

This Asiatic black bear from the Himalayas may, together with the American black bear, be a descendant of the Etruscan bear (*Ursus etruscus*) or the older species, *Ursus minimus*.

Brown bears, such as this European subspecies, originally evolved in China, subsequently spreading throughout Asia, Europe and North America. Spanish brown bears, such as this animal, are the smallest members of the species.

The polar bear is the most recently evolved bear, originating probably from a coastal population of brown bears some 3 million years ago.

The origins of the Malayan sun bear (*Ursus malayanus*) and the sloth bear (*Ursus ursinus*) are unclear. Fossil material of both of these species is very rare and neither species is known, in any form, from before the last ice age; both make their first appearance in, more or less, their current condition.

About 1 million years ago, with the retreat of the Pleistocene ice sheet, Savin's bear (*Ursus savini*) had replaced *U. etruscus* from which it had derived. This new species, known from several European sites, had a high-domed forehead and very small anterior premolar teeth. Additionally, it had carried on the trend of size increase, making it a large and impressive animal; although a cave-dweller, this was not the true cave bear but rather its direct ancestor.

THE EUROPEAN CAVE BEAR

The true cave bear of Europe (*Ursus speleaus*) can be traced back in an almost unbroken line for some 5 million years to *Ursus minimus*, the ancestor of all ursines. Etruscan bears, descending some 2.5 million years ago from *U. minimus*, were to survive only until the Late Villafranchian of Europe (*c.*1.5 million years ago), at which time they were replaced by Savin's bear (*U. savini*). In Savin's bear, known from several European sites, including England and Austria, the anterior premolar teeth had almost disappeared.

By the terminal stages of glacial advance some 800,000 years ago, a new type of (long-legged) bear had appeared. Whether this was a truly new species which had migrated across from eastern Asia or merely an open-country form of Savin's bear is not clear. Nonetheless, with the retreat of the ice sheet, true cave bears were present in Europe, together with human beings.

The first of the fully-fledged cave bears (Deninger's bear – *Ursus deningeri*) first appears during the Cromerian (1.0–0.4 million years ago). Although large, this species had not attained the size of later species and, despite possessing a longer lower jaw than *U. savini*, its molar teeth were not as expanded and its forehead not as domed as in this earlier species.

It is from deposits dating to the Holsteinian interglacial period (*c.*300,000 years ago) that the earliest definite specimens of *U. spelaeus* were recovered. This species was common in Germany, France and England; a particularly good skull was recovered from deposits at Swanscombe in Kent (southern England). This bear was large (the largest specimens were about the size of an Alaskan brown bear) and herbivorous; its large, high-domed skull sported a long jaw containing relatively enormous canine teeth. The premolar teeth were either very small or totally absent and its molars were the largest of any known bear. The exceptional wear on these back teeth, and the indications of a large, powerful jaw musculature, demonstrate the herbivorous life-style. Additionally, this bear, although possessing well-developed forelimbs, had comparatively small hind limbs; these features, plus its large size, mean that there is little possibility of its having led a predatory life-style. The large canine teeth were most probably used during competitive interactions between males. A considerable size variation of specimens has now been found to exist and is believed to indicate sexual dimorphism rather than the presence of more than one species – males being up to twice the size of females (this remains true despite considerable regional variation in overall size), a feature which, in many modern animals, correlates with strong competition between males for access to reproductive females.

Cave bears had a rather limited geographical range and, unlike brown bears, probably roamed very little. During the Late Pleistocene, with an increase in range and numbers of brown bears in Europe, cave bears started to be slowly supplanted, finally becoming extinct about 10,000 years ago.

NON-BEAR ANALOGUES

Bears were not the first mammals to evolve the large-bodied, slow-moving, omnivorous life-style; throughout the history of mammal evolution this (and other) themes have recurred time and again. Today, on all continents other than Australasia, eutherians (placentals) are the dominant type of mammal.

However, before the origin of these placentals, marsupials (metatherians) had evolved, diversified and radiated. The vagaries of continental drift isolated these animals, first in the southern hemisphere (while in the northern hemisphere they were outcompeted by the newly evolving placentals) and then in Australia. Some marsupials managed to survive the influx of placentals into South America via the Panamanian landbridge, and one, the Virginia oppossum (*Didelphis virginianus*), even managed to invade North America where it still survives today.

From early South American didelphid marsupials evolved the Borhyaenidae, which were specialized for a predatory and carnivorous life-style. Some of the earliest of the borhyaenids, such as *Borhyaena* (a wolf-like form) and *Prothylacinus* (a bear-like form), which have been recovered from Miocene deposits in Argentina, were relatively heavy-bodied, short-limbed, plantigrade animals with heavy, dog-like skulls. Despite being slow and relatively weighty, all of these animals were predominantly predatory in habit. Later borhyaenids became more specialized; the thylacosmilids of the Late Miocene and Pliocene were very similar to the eutherian sabre-toothed cats which evolved in the northern hemisphere. The advanced carnivorous specializations of genera such as *Thylacosmilus* were, however, not sufficient to enable them to effectively compete with the placental Carnivora from North America and they had all lapsed into extinction by the end of the Pliocene.

This common wombat (*Vombatus ursinus*) is an Australian marsupial which has a strong resemblance to a small bear. As a marsupial it actually has no relationship to bears at all.

Koalas (*Phascolarctos cinereus*) are so strongly reminiscent of bears that they are commonly called 'koala bears'. As with the wombat, these animals are marsupials.

An early group of eutherian mammals which would later give rise to the ancestors of the Cetacea (whales and dolphins) and ungulates (deer, antelope, etc.) were the Condylarthra. One of the earliest members of this group, *Arctocyon*, appeared some 65 million years ago; later (*c.*60 million years ago) such omnivorous arctocyonids (literally 'bear-dogs') had assumed the morphological appearance of both bears and dogs, although they had no relationship to either group.

Another eutherian group, also (confusingly) sometimes referred to as 'bear-dogs' but better known as 'half-dogs', arose from within the Carnivora as the ninth family of that order – the Amphicyonidae. True dogs (Canidae) evolved and radiated in North America before spreading out onto other continents; possibly due to competition with this group, amphicyonids are rare in North America but common in Eurasia. Throughout the European Miocene, *Amphicyon*, a large, heavily built animal, preyed on the slow-moving herbivores which flourished at that time. Some amphicyonids also pursued a bear-like, omnivorous life-style, probably in order to avoid competition with more specialist, predatory carnivores. Nonetheless, amphicyonids were eventually to lose out, in terms of size, to the bears and, in terms of speed, to the dogs, all becoming extinct some 6 million years ago.

Today there are two types of marsupial occasionally confused with bears. The first, the wombats (*Vombatus* and *Lasiorhinus* of the family Vombatidae), resemble small bears with their thick, heavy bodies, short limbs and plantigrade gait. The second, the koala (*Phascolarctos cinerea*), demonstrates some passing resemblance to a 'teddy-bear'; possibly this is the reason for it being often referred to as the 'koala bear'. Both of these animals, which seem to have some affinity with one another, are, as marsupials, totally unrelated to bears and share few ecological similarities with them.

One animal which does have some relationship to bears is the wolverine (*Gulo gulo*), which is a mustelid (and thus, like bears, an arctoid carnivore). There are two recognized subspecies, one North American and the other European, and they have a circumpolar distribution. The wolverine is a heavily built animal, with short legs and a ferocious reputation, which exists principally on a diet of flesh. During the winter, it prefers caribou and reindeer, which it is able to kill by leaping onto the back of the prey and bearing it to the ground, at which point it can deliver a powerful bite to the neck. The resemblance to a bear does not extend far; the relatively long tail of the wolverine clearly differentiating it. Indeed, despite its ferocious reputation, it is possibly killed by brown bears where their ranges overlap in North America.

Chapter 4
Food, Feeding and Energetics

The spectrum of foods available to animals fall basically into two types; other animals, and plants. Each of these foods has its own peculiar problems. Flesh is highly nutritious and easy to digest, but is difficult to catch and, in some cases, may be dangerous, possessing horns, antlers, sharp hooves and strong teeth. Plant foods are easy to harvest but are poor in nutritive terms, difficult to digest and may, in some places, be seasonally unavailable.

Although several groups of mammal have adopted a totally herbivorous diet (antelope, deer, horses, etc.), fewer are strictly carnivorous. Most carnivores have retained their vegetarian options and are really omnivorous, living on any type of food which becomes available.

DIGESTIVE ADAPTATIONS

Much can be discerned about an animal's diet from its teeth. The strict herbivores generally have sharp, high-crowned crushing and grinding teeth with which vegetation can be shredded and the tough cellulose ground down in preparation for digestion. In addition, many of these animals have teeth which grow constantly throughout their lives to compensate for the wear and tear they suffer because of the coarse vegetation diet. Carnivorous animals do not need teeth that grow on a continual basis since their teeth are not eroded to any great extent by their food. Similarly they have fewer crushing and grinding surfaces since flesh requires little in the way of preparation before entering the gut.

Most of the cats are almost totally carnivorous and, consequently, have strong shearing carnassial teeth but little else; additionally, these carnassial teeth have no discernible talonid shelf on the posterior margin (a crushing adaptation). Members of the Canidae (dogs) have retained some crushing teeth posterior to the carnassials and also have a fairly well-developed talonid shelf, features which underline the importance of vegetation in their diet. Bears, as would be expected, because of their almost total abandonment of dietary flesh, have very reduced carnassials with large talonid shelves and expanded crushing molars. The giant panda has the largest molars relative to its size of any bear, the result of its particularly difficult food staple. Polar bears have larger carnassial blades than any other species of ursid, reflecting their more predatory, flesh-eating habits.

The structure of the gut is also intimately related to the diet. Herbivorous animals often have a large chamber in which they are able to ferment their food (with the aid of symbiotic microbes); chewed food is passed to this chamber and then, after fermentation, is regurgitated for further chewing before being passed to the stomach for true digestion. Not even the most dedicated vegetarian member of the bears has evolved such a structure and bears are thus particularly inefficient at extracting nutrients from their food. This is one of the reasons why bears tend to opt for the most readily digestible available plant foods, rarely eating older grasses, sedges and leaves. Specific growth stages of plants also vary in their suitability to bears' dietary preference, even from week to week. Bears are not born with this knowledge of the temporal sequence of appropriate food; it is something which must be learned as a cub, during the time spent with its mother.

A further consequence of seasonal variability is that, in the northern hemisphere, nutritious plants may not be available during winter, forcing bears in this part of the world to spend some part of the year fasting. They cope with this by entering a period of dormancy through the cold months; at higher latitudes this may last for up to 7 months, leaving only 5 months of the year in which to feed. Consequently, every mouthful is critical and must make the maximum contribution to the year's requirements.

In addition to the multi-chambered stomach, herbivores also have very long guts which enable them to extract as great an amount of the nutrients from the food as possible. A cow has a gut some 25 times the length of its body, whereas the guts of carnivores are only about 5 times the length of their bodies; even the large size of bears does not compensate for their relatively short gut. To gain sufficient nutrients from vegetative material, bears must consequently spend a large amount of their time feeding. This is taken to the extreme in giant pandas, which spend some 12–15 hours a day consuming approximately 20 per cent of their body weight in bamboo.

DIETARY STRATEGY

A typical carnivore has to spend considerably less time feeding than does a bear but has to exert much more effort in order to secure its food. On balance, the dietary strategies adopted by both dedicated carnivores and by bears have their drawbacks and advantages. Nonetheless, bears are still faced with the serious problem of being physically incapable of meeting their dietary requirements.

Bears tend to be dietary generalists, eating almost anything, whether insect, vertebrate or vegetation. However, three species have become very specialized and have evolved adaptations allowing them to deal more efficiently with their food. Despite this, *all* bears are opportunists and will take advantage of temporal aggregations and abundance of particular foods during certain seasons; this is probably the key to their survival.

The Generalists

BROWN BEAR
Brown bears eat an enormous variety of foodstuffs. Although there are fundamental food categories adhered to over wide areas, the diet does tend to vary from region to region. Vegetative material eaten includes berries, fruit and herbage (in North America alone, more than 200 different kinds of plants are eaten). Such vegetative matter may form up to 80 per cent of the diet, with insects, fish, rodents and large mammals (such as moose, caribou, small deer and livestock) forming the remaining 20 per cent. The relative importance of meat, however, should not be underestimated; in

terms of energy, meat has a greater yield on a weight for weight basis than plants. In Tibet, brown bears are more actively predacious than in other areas and meat forms a greater proportion of the diet. In contrast, Japanese brown bears eat almost no meat; one study showed that 98.7 per cent of the diet was made up of vegetative material, particularly fruits, berries, acorns and hog's fennel. The remaining 1.3 per cent comprised flying insects that aggregate under rocks around lake shores and an occasional sample of local livestock. Brown bears living along coastlines have access to the stranded bodies of sea mammals, invertebrates (e.g. molluscs and crabs), and vegetation (e.g. seaweed).

There are apparently some fundamental differences between the foods eaten by bears in North America and by those in Eurasia. Roots and other subterranean organs of plants are more important to North American bears, whereas ants are more commonly eaten in Eurasia; this, however, appears to be more indicative of availability than preference.

In certain areas, and at certain times of year, aggregations of particular foods occur that bears are quick to take advantage of. A study in Montana revealed that brown bears feed on local aggregations of ladybirds and army cutworm moths (*Euxoa auxilaris*). Similarly, at high elevations in the Yellowstone ecosystem, bears fed on aggregations of army cutworm moths. Brown bears may also aggregate to take advantage of carcasses of large mammals, food dumps and also spawning salmon; in this latter case, bears may congregate in groups of 50 or more.

Longer-lasting seasonal changes in the types of food sought also occur. During spring insects are an important food item for bears living at high latitudes and also during summer for bears living in the Pyrenees. In Alaska, rodents become important once snow has covered the ground. Autumn is the season when bears need to fatten up in preparation for dormancy. By this time grasses have matured and are high in cellulose, making them even more difficult to digest; therefore berries, fruits and nuts become important at this time. In northern latitudes of Eurasia, fruits such as bilberry (*Vaccinium*) and crowberry (*Empetrum*) are most important. Further south, the importance of larger fruits, such as plums, pears and apples, increases and, in the far south (south of 44°N), beechnuts and acorns become the most significant fattening-up items. However, at these lower latitudes, feeding may occur throughout winter and, in this case, beech nuts and acorns remain staple food items, supplemented with some herbage.

AMERICAN BLACK BEAR

The American black bear is also primarily a vegetarian, but again will eat almost anything that comes its way. A study in the Great Smoky Mountains National Park and nearby areas, showed that 81 per cent of the diet of this bear was made up of grasses, herbs, berries and nuts. Insects, such as bees and beetles, constituted 11 per cent and the remaining percentage was household rubbish and other artificial foods. In Maine it was found that garbage assumed a greater importance, comprising as much as 15 per cent of the diet. In Washington State, skunk cabbage is eaten in large amounts (during spring) due to its abundance; in the Smoky Mountains, squawroot (a plant parasite of tree roots) is plentiful during spring and so forms a large component of the diet. The fruit of the mountain ash is eaten in large

Berries are an important component of the diets of both black and brown bears throughout autumn. Here an American black bear is feeding on blueberries, delicately using its incisor teeth to strip the berries from the stem.

amounts during summer by bears in Idaho and, in North Carolina, the fruit of the black gum tree becomes popular in autumn.

Black bears living along coastlines are also able to take advantage of fish and marine invertebrates found in tidal pools, as well as scavenging the carcasses of marine mammals. In northern Canada a population of black bears has successfully occupied a tundra habitat where they feed on lemmings; in Alaska they may hunt moose calves and salmon. Predation of young white-tailed deer is common in the Adirondack Mountains of New York State and mule deer have been observed to be taken on Vancouver Island and elk in north-central Idaho.

In spite of these regional differences, there is a general trend in the diet of black bears throughout the year. In spring, the main constituents are herbaceous plants and grasses, supplemented with carrion which has been preserved in the ice over winter. During this season bears are most likely to prey on wild animals and domestic livestock, where available, since this is the period when the most nutritious plant food is not yet in abundance and bears are at their hungriest after their long winter fast. In summer, berries become ripe and form the staple diet, which is supplemented with meat from carrion or live-caught prey. In early autumn, late-ripening berries and fruits are eaten, some bears turning to apple orchards and corn-fields for food. By late autumn, nuts become available and important as a 'fattening-up' food.

ASIATIC BLACK BEAR

As with brown and American black bears, the Asiatic black bear's diet shows both geographical and seasonal variation. Like the brown bear, this species is typically more carnivorous in India and Tibet (preying on sheep, goats and cattle) and tends toward a more vegetarian diet in Japan, a preference which leads to conflict with Japanese farmers as the bears peel away timber bark to expose the sapwood underneath.

In general, the spring diet mainly consists of succulent forbs (non-grassy, herbaceous plants) and leaves of shrubs, along with the previous autumn's acorns and beechnuts, which may have to be dug out of the ground. Bears in the mountains of the southeastern former USSR are known to lick the sap of birch trees at this time. The sap, is believed to act as a laxative, helping to expel the 'hibernation plug', a compact mass containing hair and remnants of the bear's last meal before dormancy, which remains within the colon or lower digestive tract throughout the duration of the winter sleep. By late May or early June, the first spring growth is emerging, including coltsfoot, butterbur, angelica and cow parsnip; the relative proportions and availability of each varies regionally. In summer, berries and fruits may be added to the diet; these ripen at different times depending on species and elevation (bears are always on the move at this time of year in order to be where the berries are ripening). New bamboo shoots may also be sought out, along with insects, such as ants, which can form a substantial proportion of the summer diet. In the mountainous areas of Japan, cherries, raspberries, dogwood and viburnum are the main constituents; in the Tangjiahe Reserve of northern Sichuan, China, *Rubus coreanus* berries are frequently eaten, along with wild cherries. Bird-cherries form the staple summer diet of bears in the mountains of the southeastern former USSR; there is less variety in this area than elsewhere and consequently the diet is supplemented with grass.

For this bear also, autumn is the time to fatten up in preparation for dormancy. The best fattening-up foods, which become available in the autumn, are acorns, beech nuts, cedar nuts, pine nuts, chestnuts, walnuts and hazelnuts, all of which are incredibly rich in fats and complex carbohydrates. These foods tend to grow in forests at low elevations so, by mid-September, bears are travelling downslope in order to reach them. Nuts are not the only food eaten and bears cannot rely on them alone; in certain years the crop may fail and fruit assumes a greater importance. In the Tangjiahe Reserve, acorns were the most frequently eaten autumn food, supplemented with hazelnuts, butternuts and fruits (*Celtis biondii, Actinidia chinensis*). In the southeastern former USSR, nuts are in short supply and dogwood, buckthorn and the wild grape (*Actinidia*), form a large proportion of the autumn diet.

Generally meat, either killed or scavenged, forms only a small percentage of the diet of Asiatic black bears, although they have been observed to feed on mammals, birds, fish, molluscs and insects.

SPECTACLED BEAR

For spectacled bears, variation in preferred foods has been found to be associated with both altitude and season, although the general trend is that of almost exclusive vegetarianism, with plants of the family Bromeliaceae forming as much as 50 per cent of the diet. They may also eat seasonally available fruits and berries, cacti, trees (primarily fig [*Ficus*] and *Capparis* spp.), shrubs, honey and sugar cane. The spectacled bear has extremely strong jaws which enables it to eat food that few other animals can, such as palm nuts, orchid pseudobulbs, tree bark and bromeliad hearts. It is incredibly mobile, moving from tree to tree as different fruits ripen. It may stay in one fruit tree for up to 3 or 4 days, the total ripening period, in order to take advantage of this temporary abundance, and then move on. These bears are important to the floral ecology of the forests in which they live, dispersing seeds of many trees, including laurel, for which there is only one other disperser.

As with other bears, the spectacled bear is quick to take advantage of meat, should it become available, readily feeding on mice, rabbits, deer and calves. For this they are persecuted by South American farmers.

SUN BEAR

There is comparatively little known about the diet of the sun bear, although it has been found to be an opportunistic omnivore, bees, termites, and earthworms forming the main part of its diet. Since such invertebrates are a more regular food source than fruit, this bear does not have to move about as much as the spectacled bear in order to satisfy its dietary needs. Its long tongue is ideal for extracting insects from trees and termite nests as

Bromeliads are a staple food of the spectacled bear, which is able to feed on them by virtue of its strong jaws.

well as licking honey from bee-hives. It is believed that this diet of insects is supplemented with fruits as they become available; the growing buds of coconut palms are also eaten, often causing serious damage to coconut plantations. As with other bears, should the opportunity arise, sun bears will also prey on small rodents, birds and lizards, as well as scavenging tiger kills. At human settlements they may feed on rubbish, livestock and domestic fruits, such as bananas and papayas.

The minimal seasonality of the tropics means a year-round availability of food for both sun and spectacled bears which, as a consequence, have no need to enter dormancy.

The Specialists

Sloth Bear

The main foods of the sloth bear are termites and ants, supplemented with flowers, grass and honey; between March and June fruits are included in the diet and, on occasions, may comprise as much as 50 per cent of the total food intake.

The sloth bear has adapted to cope with a diet consisting mainly of termites in a number of ways. It has a very long tongue and mobile snout which enable it to lick up insects from difficult places. An alternative method is also employed; after inserting its muzzle into a hole it has made in a termite mound, the bear blows violently to get rid of the dust and debris and then sucks in, termites being 'vacuumed' into its mouth. To

Termites are the staple food of the sloth bear. Although these insects are numerous, they are also able to produce noxious chemicals and sharp bites in defence of themselves and their mounds.

Sun bears have very long tongues which they use to collect insects and honey.

assist in this, the sloth bear has lost a pair of upper inner incisors (leaving only two pairs, separated by a median diastema through which the tongue can be protruded). In addition, the nostrils are able to close voluntarily to prevent inhalation of dust.

It is believed that the sloth bear evolved as a specialist termite-eater in order to occupy a niche which had been relatively little exploited in the region of the world in which it lives. In addition, in many areas, termites are abundant throughout the year and so provide a secure food source, meaning the bears do not have to make seasonal excursions in search of food, nor do they have to undergo a period of winter sleep to avoid times of food scarcity.

Despite this specialist tendency, it is still, like the other bears, an opportunist and, when its range encompasses human settlements, it will feed on cultivated crops, such as sugar cane and maize.

GIANT PANDA

The giant panda is a well-known specialist eater of bamboo and this plant comprises over 99 per cent of its diet. So far, records show that at least 30 species of the plant are utilized. The species eaten vary from region to region, although, in general, umbrella bamboo (*Fargesia spatheca*, also recorded as *F. robusta*) and arrow bamboo (*Sinarundinaria chungi*, *S. nitida* and *S. fangiana*) are the most important. Up to 25 other wild plant species may also occasionally be eaten, including *Potamogeton* (a water weed), *Actinidia* (a vine), juniper (*Juniperus* spp.), dragon spruce (*Picea asperata*), holly (*Ilex franchetiana*) and wild parsnip (*Angelica* spp.).

The fact that meat forms an almost negligible part of the diet is more likely due to lack of availability and opportunity; pandas make clumsy predators and easy prey is scarce. Very few large predators overlap the panda's range and, consequently, there is little to scavenge. In contrast, bamboo is extremely abundant, as well as being easy to harvest.

Over time, the body of the panda has become adapted to this diet of bamboo. One obvious adaptation is the development and elongation of the radial sesamoid to form a sixth digit which allows increased dexterity while handling the bamboo. The skull has a large sagittal crest and has become wider and deeper. These modifications allow for a greater surface area for attachment of the masticatory muscles, which are also very well developed, thus producing powerful jaws. In addition, the molar and premolar teeth are wider and flatter than those of other bears and have developed extensive ridges and cusps in order to grind the fibrous plant material. The gullet is particularly tough and the stomach walls are extremely muscular: adaptations to squeeze and churn the woody bamboo fragments. The gut is protected from bamboo splinters by a thick layer of mucus, produced by the copious mucous cells in the walls.

However, despite these adaptations, the panda, like other bears, still retains the simple digestive tract of a carnivore, with no special chamber to retain food and no symbiotic bacteria to digest cellulose and hemicelluloses. Digestion of bamboo (which is low in nutrients anyway, containing high levels of indigestible cellulose and lignin [35–65 per cent] and partially digestible hemicelluloses [20–35 per cent]) is therefore very inefficient. Studies indicate that pandas are able to digest only approximately 20 per cent of the dry matter of bamboo (for a typical herbivore this figure is closer to 80 per cent). Bamboo thus passes through the gut virtually undigested and, consequently, pandas must eat large amounts of food just to sustain body maintenance and growth. Since so little can be extracted from the bamboo, it has to be passed through the gut quickly to allow room for the next meal; the gut passage time of bamboo for giant pandas is approximately 14 hours, much faster than the times given for an average meal of other carnivores.

To maximize nutrient intake, pandas need to harvest bamboo selectively for the most nutritious parts and are known to discard certain items on the basis of their smell. Schaller and co-workers found that, in general, and for most of the year, leaves were favoured over other parts. Leaves contain the most protein and least cellulose; Schaller believes the latter to be the most likely selecting factor. However, for some hitherto unexplained reason, leaves are not eaten during the spring, although their protein and cellulose levels are consistent throughout the year. Logically, pandas select thick shoots over thin ones; it takes as least as much effort to remove the sheaths from a thin shoot as from a thick one, but the rewards are much greater from the latter. They also tend not to eat short shoots (less than 25cm/ 10in long) as these consist almost entirely of sheaths. A panda will often forage along the edge of thickets, or in small patches, as shoot density is greater around the edge of a thicket and thin shoots are significantly more common inside a stand.

Pandas usually feed sitting upright, so that the forelegs are free to manipulate the bamboo stalks. The bamboo stem is then grasped and bent

Giant pandas spend the majority of their time feeding; although bamboo is the principal component of their diet, this animal is eating meat.

sideways using the forepaws and bitten off fairly close to the base. The woody sheath of older stems is removed by biting into the base with the incisors and tearing strips off by simultaneously twisting paw and head in opposite directions. The stem is then pushed at right angles into the corner of the mouth, the panda rapidly biting at the same time, jerking the forepaw and moving the head, helping to sever the stem. The amount of time a panda spends feeding in one particular place varies considerably; they may subsist for months within 1km² (247 acres).

POLAR BEAR

The polar bear is unique among the bears in that it has, secondarily, assumed a more carnivorous life-style. The winter diet consists predominantly of ringed seals (*Phoca hispida*), which are abundant in the Arctic; less abundant, and consequently less preyed upon, are bearded seals (*Erignathus barbatus*). This diet of seals is supplemented with fish, crabs and carrion. Populations in certain areas may also prey on young walrus, beluga and narwhal, although this is considered rare.

Polar bears have high digestive efficiencies for the principle dietary components of protein and fat and are able to assimilate approximately 84 per cent of the protein ingested and approximately 97 per cent of the fat. This extremely high digestive efficiency of fat means that a polar bear may very often eat only the blubber of a seal, taking time to shear off the meat with its incisors; however, a hungry bear, or a female with cubs, will eat the meat as well. Unless a bear is starving, it will not eat the hair or bone since these are virtually indigestible and have also been proven to reduce the overall digestibility of protein. There is rarely any waste though;

Ringed seals (*Phoca hispida*) between the ages of 6 months and 2 years are the major part of the diet of polar bears.

scavengers abound in the Arctic and gulls, ravens, Arctic foxes and subadult polar bears are always on hand to take advantage of leftovers.

Polar bears have huge stomachs, enabling them to take advantage of any temporary windfall; they are able to eat up to 20 per cent of their body weight in a single sitting. One report states that the average active polar bear needs approximately 2kg (4¼lb) of seal fat per day to survive. Any seal over 1 month old could therefore satisfy a polar bear's daily needs and an adult ringed seal could provide enough energy for about 11 days. It has been shown that seals between 6 months and 2 years of age comprise at least half the seals killed by these bears. Although subadult seals provide less food, the bear is more certain of capture as young seals are less experienced and wary than adults. Very young seals (less than 1 month old) are abandoned if incidently killed, as they provide too little return.

During summer, the sea ice melts, limiting the bear's access to seals. In some regions, such as the western Arctic, bears are able to migrate with the retreating ice, thus reducing their period without seals. However, at Hudson Bay, the sea ice melts completely for about 4 months every year and the bears must subsist primarily on stored fat, supplemented with grass, berries and algae, which may perhaps be a source of essential minerals. Bears at Churchill (western Hudson Bay) have also learned to feed at the garbage dump and, although studies have shown that bears feeding at the dump were indeed heavier than other bears, this supplementary feeding seemed not to provide any reproductive or survival advantage.

Predatory Behaviour

During winter and spring, polar bears generally only have access to seals through breathing-holes (which at this time of year are hidden under snow-drifts) and birthing-lairs (which are excavated out of snow which has accumulated over the breathing-holes). The main technique employed is that known as 'still-hunting', in which a bear waits motionless (either lying down or standing) at a breathing-hole or birthing-lair, sometimes for many hours, until it hears or smells a seal surfacing to breathe. At this point it attacks, breaking through the snowdrift to grasp the seal with the jaws. If the hole is located deep under the snow, the bear may first excavate a hole and lie with its head down this hole, waiting for the seal. Alternatively, a seal under a snowdrift may be detected from some distance away, in which case, the bear approaches very slowly and attacks immediately.

In summer, seals may haul out at the now uncovered breathing-holes, and at cracks which form in the ice as it begins to melt. Again, however, the commonest method employed by the bears is still-hunting. A polar bear traverses the ice, sniffing at possible haul-out places. If it detects seal scent it begins its wait, the most usual position being on the stomach, with the chin close to the edge of the ice. This position conserves energy and also presents the lowest silhouette against the sky to any seal below. When a seal surfaces, the bear grasps it around the upper body with its teeth and flips it out onto the ice, where bites to the head are used to kill it before it is dragged away from the water and eaten. At this time of year, polar bears may also stalk basking seals; this has to be done with extreme caution as seals are quite alert while on the ice, lifting their heads and scanning for

In summer, 'leads' that form as the ice melts are ideal hunting spots for polar bears. This particular polar bear may wait here for many hours until a seal surfaces. Alternatively it may use the 'lead' as cover to swim closer to a seal that it has spotted from a distance.

predators regularly. A bear lowers its head, sometimes assuming a semi-crouched position, and walks very slowly towards the seal; once within 20m (22yd) or so it charges at amazing speed. Another form of this type of hunting occurs in the water and is known as the 'aquatic stalk'; it is a very specialized method and practised by only a few bears. Before entering the water, the bear memorizes the route; once in the water it then remains totally submerged (apart from its nose breaking the surface occasionally to enable it to breathe) until the seal is reached, at which point the bear explodes from the water and attacks.

The success of polar-bear hunts varies greatly, depending on the prevailing ice conditions; the most successful occur in areas of active or moving pack ice and along the edge of the fast ice or floes. The least successful hunts occur on the hummocky fast ice. Success also depends, of course, on individual bears. In general though, less than 15 per cent of attempts prove successful. Consequently, a polar bear must spend at least half its time hunting. Once a seal has been killed it is eaten immediately; there is no evidence to show that polar bears cache their food.

Cubs do not instinctively know how to hunt; this is a skill which they must learn from their mothers. By the time they are 1 year old, cubs may be hunting for approximately 4 per cent of the time. This figure increases to 7 per cent by the time they are 2 years old, killing a seal every 5–6 days; at this age they are ranging further from their mother and are choosing their hunting-sites independently.

Although principally vegetarian, brown bears are able to hunt for food when the opportunity arises. By using their considerable bulk and strong jaws, brown bears are able to kill animals as large as caribou. Observing such hunts provides valuable learning experience for cubs.

In certain areas and at certain times of year, rodents may comprise an important part of the diet of both brown and black bears. Typically, small rodents are killed with a swat of the paw.

It is not advantageous for polar bears to hunt in groups because of the relatively small size of their main prey, ringed seals. Also, the paucity of larger prey does not stimulate the development of group-hunting. The same is true of the other bears; if they hunted in groups they would have to travel great distances since prey density is so low. Long-distance travel by bears is very costly, as well as being slow, and, if the kill had to be shared, the return would be relatively less. Thus, bears are solitary hunters.

Due to the high cost of locomotion, running after prey is only cost-efficient if the prey is caught quickly (brown bears are able to run in short bursts for 1 or 2km [about 1 mile] and even reach speeds of up to 50km/h [30mph]. Thus, they must be highly selective about what, and where, they hunt; deer calves, too young to run, are prime targets. On the European taiga, successful predation of moose occurs where there is a frozen snow crust; this makes it difficult for the deer to move, but does not impede bears. Caribou are also very often taken, usually by ambush.

The size of the bear obviously affects the size of the prey it can hunt. Brown bears are able to prey on moose (*Alces alces*), wapiti or elk (*Cervus canadensis*), caribou or reindeer (*Rangifer tarandus*), bison (*Bison bison* and *B. bonasus*) and musk ox (*Ovibos moschatus*); black bears, being smaller, more commonly take calves of white-tailed deer (*Odocoileus virginianus*) and moose. Black bears living on the tundra of northern Labrador prey on the large numbers of small mammals available (lemmings and voles) and, in Alaska, feed on snowshoe hares (*Lepus americanus*).

Both species may also feed on rodents and fish. Black bears have been observed killing mice by slapping at them with a paw, thereby crushing the prey. A variety of techniques is used to catch fish and each bear has its own individual style. A commonly employed method is to plunge headfirst into the river from land and grab a fish with the front paws or the jaws; inexperienced bears may land with a 'belly flop' (thereby scaring all the fish away!). Alternatively, a bear may use the centre of the river as a place of attack, sometimes even swimming under water, rushing at the fish with jaws open. At places where fish are able to jump clear of the rapids, bears may wait and snap the fish out of the air with paws or jaws. At salmon spawning-grounds, fish may be particularly numerous and up to 20 salmon may be caught in an hour. Under such circumstances, only the most nutritious parts are eaten: the brain and, if the fish is female, the eggs.

Unlike the polar bear, brown bears are known to cache carcasses. The kill is hidden under dirt and leaves and very often the bear resides at the cache site, presumably to guard it.

Almost nothing is known of the predatory behaviour of the other bear species. There are accounts of giant pandas hunting bamboo rats; after locating the rat's burrow, the panda stomps on the ground and catches the rat in its mouth as it runs out.

Cannibalism among temperate and Arctic species is known to occur, although it is thought to be relatively rare. The ecological significance of this is, as yet, unclear; it may just be the activity of starving bears that are likely to eat anything they come across. Infanticide, however, does have an explanation in that, if cubs are killed in spring by an adult male, the female may come into oestrus again and be able to produce his offspring. This is only beneficial to males if they are able to recognize, and therefore not kill, their own offspring and also if they have a high chance of mating with

Bears may congregate at rich food sources. Here, brown bears have come together to fish at the Brooks River in Katmei National Park, Alaska.

The relative scarcity of large food items, such as this deer carcass, means that it is beneficial for bears to hide such items from scavengers and other predators.

the female when she becomes receptive. Clearly, there are no benefits to females from this behaviour and they defend their cubs fiercely. Brown-bear predation of black bears is also known to occur.

The bear most likely to kill human beings for food is the polar bear, since, to this bear, anything which is encountered in the barren landscape of the Arctic is likely to be potential food. Attacks on human beings by other species of bear do not usually lead to the body being eaten; they most often occur when bears are startled or frightened.

Feeding Signs

Brown bears have large claws and a large shoulder musculature adapted for digging food out of the ground, whether it be roots, tubers or rodents. Once a bear has dug deep enough it peels back the earth to expose the meal. Consequently a meadow in which a bear has been digging looks like it has been ploughed. Brown bears and black bears may also overturn rocks and ants' nests in the search for food; evidence of bear activity can be determined by the fact that the ground underneath will show characteristic claw marks.

American and Asiatic black bears have shorter, more curved claws which allow them to feed on nuts and fruit in trees. Nuts are clasped with the lips, whereas berries are grasped with the teeth; paws are used to bend the food-laden branches towards the animal. As broken branches accumulate under the bear, a characteristic 'nest' is formed which may be used to determine where a bear has been feeding; in Japan these are known as *enza*. Spectacled bears may purposely build feeding platforms in fruit trees if the branches are not strong enough to support their weight. These may be about 6m by 5m (20ft by 16ft) in size and several leaf layers may be added as bedding. These 'day beds' may be used for quite a while, as evidenced by the large numbers of bear droppings often found close by.

Droppings, in fact, are the best indication of what any bear has been eating, and where, and are important in many scientific studies.

Activity

Brown bears may be active at any time of day or night, although they are more likely to be active around dawn and dusk and may be nocturnal in areas where there is a lot of human activity.

It was once believed that all American black bears were nocturnal, probably due to the fact that they kept their daily activities hidden from human researchers. With the advent of radio-telemetry, it has become evident that some black bears are active during the day and may, in fact, change their activity pattern according to season. One study of black bears in the Great Smoky Mountains National Park showed that, in spring, bears were crepuscular (active at dawn and dusk); in summer they also became active in the middle of the day and, in autumn, they were as active by day as by night. It was concluded that changes in activity were related to food supply. In spring, bears weigh very little, having used their fat reserves during hibernation; in addition, there is very little nutritious food available. Consequently, the bears need to conserve energy and do this by eating for only part of the day, resting for the remainder of the time. In summer, there is a plentiful supply of food, so bears spend more of their time eating and, in autumn, food is abundant and the bears' aim is to put on as much weight as possible before the onset of winter so they spend virtually all of their time eating.

Asiatic black bears are typically nocturnal, but, in some areas, they may be active during the day as well. In the Tangjiahe Reserve, activity levels were found to be higher on moonlit nights. Polar bears also tend to be more active at night and it is thought that this is related to the behaviour of seals, which feed at night as their prey tends to move closer to the surface of the water at this time.

Spectacled, sun and sloth bears are generally believed to be nocturnal, although a female sloth bear with cubs may feed more during the day, possibly to avoid nocturnal predators, such as tigers, leopards and other bears. Giant pandas may be active at any time of the day or night.

ENERGETICS

Energy is acquired from food and, in addition to its being used for general body maintenance, it is also expended during moving around, reproducing, growth and the acquiring and keeping of resources. Animals have to match their intake of food (and thus energy) with their requirements much in the same way that we have to balance income with outgoings in our bank accounts. The price of failure in animals, however, is more severe than a letter of reprimand from the bank manager!

Energy expenditure is greatest among *endotherms*; the maintenance of a constant body temperature is very costly since heat is generated internally rather than being absorbed from the environment, as is the case in *ectotherms*. Energy expenditure is also high when animals have high activity levels (and may result from either being active for long periods of time or using expensive forms of locomotion, such as flight), expensive means of resource acquisition or the need to retain such resources for extended periods of time, high reproductive rates, high post-natal growth rates and extended periods of parental care of offspring (production of milk, carrying and protecting young, etc.). Bears clearly fulfill some of these features and are thus expected to have quite considerable energy requirements.

Prior to entering their winter dens, bears put on as much weight as they can, becoming, in some cases, incredibly obese.

Some factors of an animal's biology seem to affect all aspects of energy expenditure; large size, for instance, generally increases the energy budget of an animal. Other aspects of biology, such as whether an animal is a hunter or a grazer, although still affecting the overall energy expenditure, does so by acting selectively on certain activities, rather than continuously on all activities; for instance, being a predator increases energy demands during predation but not during sleep.

Clearly, there are many variables which affect energy use by animals and these are likely to vary in importance between species. What is needed is some measure of energy expenditure by which animals can be compared and which standardizes all the variables experienced by different animals under different conditions. The basal metabolic rate (BMR) is such a measure which is equivalent across species and thus allows for direct comparisons. This quantifies the minimum cost of maintenance at normal body temperature in a fed, adult animal.

Body mass is generally regarded as one of the most important determinants of BMR in mammals (as size decreases, BMR increases); some researchers consider it to be the only such determinant. When metabolic rates are examined for members of the Carnivora it is found that body mass is indeed significant. If the BMR is measured in terms of the volume of oxygen used per unit of body mass then (among carnivores), this oxygen demand can be calculated from the expression $4.05\,m^{-0.288}$ (where m = mass). This means that the product of the body mass of the animal under consideration raised to the power -0.288 and the value 4.05 predicts the volume of oxygen (VO_2) required for an individual of that mass. Other such expressions have been derived by experimentation, e.g. the Kleiber equation ($VO_2 = 3.42\,m^{-0.25}$), which predicts an oxygen requirement slightly higher than that predicted by the equation above.

When mammals as a whole are treated in this fashion another equation is derived from which can be determined the mean mammalian curve, i.e. an expression which relates body mass and metabolic rate for all mammals. In this equation the volume of oxygen required per unit mass is given by the term $3.45\,m^{-0.287}$; this value (for mammals as a whole) is 17 per cent lower than that derived for the Carnivora from the first expression ($4.05\,m^{-0.288}$). Consideration of members of the Carnivora alone, however, is not this clear-cut and individual species may fall quite considerable distances away from the line described by the equation $VO_2 = 3.45\,m^{-0.287}$. In fact, the spread is very large: basal metabolic variation between 41 per cent and 244 per cent of that predicted on the basis of body mass accounts for only 68 per cent of the species of the order; the remaining 32 per cent shows even greater divergence from the prediction.

When bears are considered by themselves, the deviation away from the predicted values is much less, only between 80 per cent and 115 per cent of the expected value. However, this is almost certainly an oversimplification for these animals since there is little data to work with, only three species having been investigated (polar, brown and American black bears).

Another potential factor influencing BMR is diet. It is generally true that, for animals with masses in excess of 100g (3½oz), predators and grazers have basal rates of metabolism which are greater than, or the same as, those predicted by the Kleiber equation. Animals which feed on invertebrates, fruits or leaves, on the other hand, have basal metabolic rates lower than those calculated from this expression. Species with mixed diets tend to have intermediate basal rates. These effects of food on basal metabolism have been identified as resulting from one of two conditions. Firstly there are certain food-habit factors which restrict the availability of energy and these are associated with low metabolic rates. On the other hand, there are food-habit factors which do not restrict energy acquisition and these permit (but do not necessarily require) high rates of metabolism.

Factors which may act to impede high rates of energy intake include low nutrient (or energy) contents of food and seasonal variations in the availability of food; both of these features are of importance to bears. Termites (one of the staple foods of sloth bears) are generally low in nutrients, as is bamboo, the preferred food of the giant panda. Seasonal variations in the availability of food is a serious factor affecting bears at high latitudes where, for some part of the year, food becomes very scarce or even unavailable altogether. These conditions are exacerbated in bears which, as large animals, have to eat large amounts of food anyway in order to meet their general maintenance needs.

Bears do indeed have metabolic rates which reflect their diets: the polar bear, which subsists almost totally on meat, has a high metabolic rate; brown bears, which have a mixed diet, have intermediate metabolic rates; and American black bears, which have the most vegetarian diet of these three species, also have the lowest BMR. The sloth bear has a BMR similar to that of the American black bear; again, a diet-related rate since the vertebrate component of the diet of sloth bears is also negligible. Although activity

The long pelt of the sloth bear may be an adaptation to overcome cold. Although these bears live in the tropics, their food is of such poor energy value that they may be prone to cold stress.

increases the metabolic rate of sloth bears, the factor which causes the greatest rise is cold: at ambient temperatures of less than 10°C (50°F), the metabolic rate may rise to between 200 and 700 per cent of its resting level merely to maintain the animal's core temperature. Feeding increases the metabolic rate by only about 30 per cent of its resting value, due to the fact that termites comprise about 50 per cent of the diet of this bear, the remainder being mostly fruit. It has been suggested that the exclusively tropical distribution and heavy coat of long hair sported by sloth bears may be adaptations which help overcome the thermal problems associated with the low-metabolic-rate diet which they prefer.

A final ecological factor which may have important consequences for the BMR of bears is climate. Broadly speaking, it has been found that animals living in cold climates have high metabolic rates, whereas those living in warm climates have lower basal metabolisms. Although this may not seem too surprising, it has to be noted that there are a large number of exceptions to this generalization. In addition it is also often difficult to separate the effects of climate from those of food. The food-determined metabolic rates of the three species of bear given above could equally well be climatically determined since the polar bear, with the highest rate, lives in the cold and the American black bear, with the lowest rate, lives in much warmer areas; brown bears, inhabiting areas of intermediate climate, have intermediate metabolic rates.

Giant pandas have a very strict energy budget which allows for little error and, correspondingly, they have reduced their energy expenditure to a minimum; they spend a lot of time in repose, travel as little as possible and predominantly indulge in the activity of foraging. It has been calculated that the average energy expenditure for a 100kg (220lb) giant panda is about 9.2MJ/day (2,200kcal/day); this is a resting requirement and takes no account of reproduction and growth. Bamboo, with negligible differences between species, is basically a very poor nutritional source. However, it is abundant and it is also present all year round (features not necessarily true of the foods of other bears). Once the energy costs of growth and reproduction are taken into account, the daily energy requirement has risen to about 16.7MJ/day (4,000 kcal/day), some 1.4 times the BMR of this bear. With bamboo providing, on average, 22.5MJ/day (5,400kcal/day), based on the animals feeding maximally, it is clear that pandas have little room for extra burdens.

The feeding strategies of giant pandas and other bears represent two very different solutions to their energy requirements: whereas pandas have opted for stable, low quality foods, other bears have taken the route of more nutritious foods which are temporally unpredictable. The more risky strategy of bears in general has required that some species spend a considerable part of the year in a state where food is not needed. This does, however, mean that they have to prepare for this period during those times of the year when food is abundant.

Weight Gain

The amount of weight gained by brown and black bears just before hibernation can be phenomenal. A large brown bear may consume as much as

41kg (90lb) of food a day and gain approximately 2–3kg (4½–6½lb) of fat every 24 hours. At this rate of gain, they may achieve an average protective fat layer of 5cm (2in) to take into hibernation with them. American black bears may gain 0.5–1.5kg (1–3¼lb) per day in weight during autumn, which may provide sufficient energy to allow them to survive about 5 days of torpor. It has been suggested that, in grizzly bears, the evolution of a few morphological adaptations to herbivory and the conservation of the physiological adaptations of carnivory combine to make possible the rapid weight gains that occur before denning. This assumes an evolutionary trade-off between the ability to digest food rapidly (a trait of carnivores) and the ability to digest low-quality food efficiently (a trait of herbivores). The conclusion is that rapid processing at the expense of efficient digestion of fibre allows bears to take advantage of the large amounts of food available during the foraging period. One study carried out on black bears showed that, in fact, a change in digestion occurs which enables this rapid weight gain in the autumn: there is an increase in fat and carbohydrate assimilation at the expense of protein assimilation.

Bears very rarely have to chase their food and have no natural enemies, therefore agility and swiftness are not overly important to them and they can afford to put on considerable amounts of weight. Fat is distributed mainly around the hips and thighs (as in human females) and it is thought that this is an adaptation allowing them to undergo bouts of extreme obesity. This is due to the fact that storing fat in the abdominal cavity (as in human males) is physiologically more harmful. Another adaptation concerns the properties of the adipocytes, cells in which fat is stored. In most mammals, these increase in number as fat levels rise. In bears, however, the cell number remains relatively constant, but the adipocytes increase in volume as more fat is ingested.

Storing large amounts of fat means that bears are at risk from certain pollutants. Polar bears are most susceptible because of their place at the top of the marine food chain. However, all bears that accumulate large fat reserves are very vulnerable to contamination since many poisonous chemicals are fat-soluble and so become concentrated in fatty tissue when ingested, remaining inert until the bear draws on its fat reserves during winter hibernation or summer fasting. This is particularly dangerous to pregnant females (which undergo gestation and parturition while fasting). Fat-soluble contaminants released during gestation may affect foetal development and, once the cubs are born, fats (containing contaminants) in the mother's milk may further affect the growth of the young bears. As yet, there has been relatively little research into how pollutants may interfere in this way and so it is unknown how severely bears may be affected.

Thermoregulation

Mammals are warm-blooded animals (endotherms), i.e. they produce heat internally and maintain a more or less constant body temperature in the face of widely fluctuating environmental temperatures. This contrasts with cold-blooded animals (ectotherms), such as lizards, which heat their bodies up in the sun's rays; their body temperature is thus rather dependent on

Polar bears are remarkably well adapted for life in the Arctic regions; the thick layer of subcutaneous fat means that they can even swim in subzero waters without suffering hypothermia.

the temperature of their surroundings (this is the reason why there are no lizards in the Arctic and Antarctic). The production of internal heat by mammals makes them very susceptible to overheating; indeed it is generally more difficult for a mammal to prevent overheating than it is to prevent freezing. This is doubly true for large-bodied animals in which the ratio of their surface area to their volume (the SA: Vol ratio) is low (a consequence of volume increasing at a greater rate than surface area, with the same increase in the linear dimensions; volume increases as length^3 whereas surface area increases as length^2). This means that the heat-generating volume of the animal increases faster than the surface area available for the dissipation of this heat; therefore low SA: Vol ratios favour heat retention.

It might be expected that this would be of great importance to polar bears living in the extreme cold of the Arctic wastes. In practice this is not so; these bears have additional adaptations which prevent heat loss and, so efficient are these, that this species is liable to overheat very quickly with the least exertion. One such adaptation is a layer of subcutaneous blubber which may be up to 11 cm (4½in) thick; the heat conductivity of fatty tissues is so low that this forms a very efficient insulation.

Coloration too is important; it is well known that dark colours tend to absorb heat whereas light colours tend to reflect it. In giant pandas the black coloration of the ears may well be important in the reduction of heat loss across them (although this does not help explain the dark patches elsewhere on their bodies which, since they do not protrude, are unlikely to be areas through which heat may be lost). The white coloration of polar bears may therefore exist to prevent excessive heat uptake and, although it is true that considerable amounts of heat will be reflected by the white colour, this is not the whole story since polar bears are not really white! The hairs in the coat of a polar bear are hollow and it is for this reason that they appear to be white; in fact they are colourless and, being hollow, serve to conduct heat down the shaft to the skin, which is black and therefore a good absorber of heat.

Clearly polar bears are designed to be comfortable at low temperatures, the lower the better in fact. For bears, and mammals in general, the normal resting body temperature is $37\,^{\circ}$C ($98.6\,^{\circ}$F) and this is maintained by metabolic processes. The body temperature and metabolic rate of a polar bear remain at normal levels at ambient temperatures down to $-37\,^{\circ}$C ($-34\,^{\circ}$F). The highly effective insulation means that, at these temperatures, no extra energy expenditure is required for the animal to stay within its normal thermal limits so long as the animal stays relatively inactive and out of cold winds. During the summer months of July and August, when polar bears are found at more southerly latitudes where the ambient temperatures may be as high as 20–$30\,^{\circ}$C (68–$86\,^{\circ}$F), they have to cope with the problems of heat stress.

One way to avoid overheating would be to remain inactive; this is clearly not a viable option, but if activity is kept to a minimum, the chances of suffering heat stress are considerably reduced. Polar bears have been found to be able to keep their body temperature within its normal limits at environmental temperatures of -15 to $-25\,^{\circ}$C (5 to $-13\,^{\circ}$F) if they keep their walking speed down to less than about 4km (2.5mph). If they speed up to about 7 km/h (4mph), then their body temperature rises to about $39\,^{\circ}$C ($102\,^{\circ}$F) – what we would consider to be a fever! In addition, it is necessary for the bear to use more than 10 times the amount of energy it would use during resting in order to move at this speed. So, polar bears can minimize their chances of succumbing to heat stress by moving at slow speeds which are within the energetically efficient range. This makes it clear why polar bears normally tend to travel at a relatively moderate pace and why still-hunting is the most popular hunting method used.

Another behavioural means by which heat may be reduced is to enter the water; so efficient is the insulation of the polar bear, that it has little fear of freezing, even in the subzero Arctic waters. The thermal conductivity of water is some 20 times greater than that of air and thus allows rapid cooling. Cubs less than about 6 months old, however, can easily cool too much if they enter the water; they are small and, although the SA: Vol ratio is low, it is not as low as that of an adult. Furthermore, they have not yet developed sufficient insulation. Consequently, it is rare to see a female try to take young cubs into the water. Once past 6 months of age, the chances of over-cooling are much reduced and cubs enter water quite readily.

In addition to these behavioural thermoregulatory options, polar bears are also physiologically equipped for heat stress. Excess heat can be readily lost from areas of the body where blood vessels come close to the surface of the skin and are thus subject to a thermal gradient. Bears seem to have several such areas where warm blood from deep within the body is brought close to the surface: the muzzle, nose and footpads are obvious, by virtue of their lack of fur and subcutaneous insulation. The ears can also be used

Polar bears are so well insulated against the cold of their environment that they are more in danger of overheating than overcooling. This is such a problem for the bears that they have to spend some time cooling off.

as heat-exchangers because they protrude from the top of the head. In addition, there is an area inside the top of the thighs which is usually sparsely furred; when bears rest or sleep they may lay sprawled out on their backs, with their feet in the air and the insides of their thighs exposed to the cooling wind. If, on the other hand, they do not need to cool down, they huddle themselves into a ball, often hiding areas such as the nose and muzzle with their paws.

Internally, both the brain and lungs are susceptible to temperature extremes. The problem of overheating the brain is faced by many animals living in extreme climates (hot or cold) since blood passing to the brain from the body will be warm and in need of cooling. Most animals have solved this problem by use of a counter-current heat-exchange mechanism in which the warm, arterial blood entering the brain is cooled as the internal carotid artery passes close to a network of cooler, venous vessels. In bears, the artery actually bends back on itself so that it can get the best out of this close apposition with the veins. A somewhat similar mechanism exists in the nasal cavity, where the highly folded turbinal bones of the skull are overlain by a thin sheet of moist, mucous membrane. Here, warm air leaving the lungs loses some of its heat and water while cold air entering from the outside is warmed and moistened. Both of these effects are the product of gradients of heat and water between the blood vessels in the mucosa and the air passing through the nasal passage.

Thermoregulation is an extreme problem for very young animals. Bears are born in a highly altricial state – i.e. almost naked, blind and helpless. Their small size and lack of fur mean that they are immediately subject to rapid cooling; in addition they are wet from the birth membranes and have

Bears are born naked and helpless and, therefore thermally incompetent; they are totally dependent on the body warmth provided by their mothers and the den for the first few weeks of life. By 10 days they have a thin fur coat although their eyes are still closed.

no insulating layer of fatty tissue. The mother has already minimized the risks considerably by giving birth in a den, where the temperature is higher than that of the environment; nonetheless, it is still too cold for the young to survive without help. The female cleans and dries the infant and then huddles it close to her own body. The infant stays in close contact with its mother for a considerable time, until it is more able to cope with the cold. Although bears are usually described as being born naked, they do have a light covering of hair which will act as an effective, warm boundary layer next to the skin. Unfortunately, neonate mammals do not generally have the nervous co-ordination necessary for shivering (a form of muscular work which generates heat) and, despite the actions of the mother, infants may still be in serious danger of freezing.

However, young mammals are not totally defenceless in this respect since they are usually supplied with areas of a special type of fatty deposit called brown adipose tissue (BAT). This type of fatty tissue differs from the white adipose tissue (WAT) in that it is purely thermogenic in function: key biochemical processes in the tissues have become uncoupled from their normal activities and produce heat instead. This is critical to very young animals and, after a certain age, this function ceases as more standard methods of heat generation take over.

Winter Dormancy

It is common for temperate species of bear to enter a period of dormancy during winter when there is little food available. This is not the case for all subspecies or individuals, however, for it is dependent on age, sex, reproductive status and latitude. Male polar bears and all tropical species do not enter into this prolonged torpid state, but females of all species, including those of tropical distribution, do remove themselves to a den for the purposes of gestation and birth. For most species this period is characterized by fasting and therefore differs little from the dormancy of the high-latitude species. The giant panda is unique among bears in that neither sex undergoes a period of prolonged fasting. Their staple food is abundant all year round and females have no need to enter into starvation during their period of pregnancy.

This period of winter dormancy is often referred to as 'hibernation', but this is not really accurate because hibernation involves considerable reductions in metabolic processes, heart rate and body temperature. Some bats and various other small mammals do undergo such physiological changes; bears on the other hand seem not to. Although there may be small changes in heart and metabolic rates, most research suggests that these are nowhere as significant as those of true hibernators. Nonetheless, research is equivocal on this fact and one study on the American black bear described the heart rate dropping from the normal resting rate of about 40 beats per minute down to 8. Female bears, which may enter this period of dormancy pregnant, do not really have much leeway in this respect since radical physiological changes may compromise the chances of successful birth.

True hibernators wake up periodically (every 4–10 days) in order to void waste products and, occasionally, to feed and, as with the commencement of hibernation, they return to this state rapidly after these brief forays. In contrast, bears enter dormancy slowly and do not awake unless disturbed (dormant bears are easily aroused, unlike true hibernators); furthermore, bears do not feed or excrete waste products during the period of their winter sleep. It might be expected that they would emerge after this period in a state of severe emaciation and toxic stress brought on by the accumulation of waste products in their bodies (since they have not altered their rate of metabolic activity to any great extent). That this is not the case underlines some impressive physiological mechanisms used by bears during this period.

Bears do emerge from torpor much thinner than they enter it, but this reduction is almost totally accounted for by loss of fat; the muscle bulk stays more or less constant throughout. Before entering their winter dens, bears gorge on seasonally abundant foods, storing up large fat reserves to tide them over the lean period. Each day preceding dormancy a bear has to eat enough high-energy foods to satisfy both its current (active) and future (resting) metabolic needs. The majority of any excess accumulates as fat and, by the time the animal emerges from its den, it will have lost between 25 and 45 per cent of its bulk by burning this fat to fuel its metabolism and provide its fluid needs.

The use of fat as a metabolic fuel is not unusual in itself; all mammals are able to utilize it. However, the commoner fuel is glucose, even though fat, in terms of energy provided by its combustion, is superior and, in addition, produces water when broken down. Given these facts it is surprising that mammals do not use fat catabolism more than they do. The reason for this is that fats are unable to meet all of the demands of the mammalian body. The brain is unable to utilize any food source other than glucose without suffering some problems and foetuses are totally unable to utilize fatty acids as fuel; they must have glucose. For a fasting mammal, this glucose demand can be met by breakdown of muscle proteins. Starvation initiates this form of sugar production in most mammals but the body is unable to maintain it for very long before becoming critically emaciated. If this were true of bears they would have become extinct long ago; females breaking down proteins to feed foetuses would rapidly become unable to support pregnancy and abort. However, bears have evolved a remarkable physiological recycling mechanism to overcome this: urea, one of the waste products of protein breakdown, is hydrolysed and the nitrogen so produced is combined with glycerol to produce amino acids, the basic components of proteins. Thus, by breaking down protein, a bear is able to meet its demand for glucose and, by the hydrolysis of urea, maintain its muscle mass throughout the period of starvation.

The metabolic demands of gestation and lactation are difficult to meet in the den; lactation is very expensive to females. Fortunately, newborn animals are able to utilize fatty acids in the way that foetuses are not; shortening the true gestation period allows female bears to cut down on the amount of protein breakdown they have to undergo to produce glucose. All bears have short gestation periods for their body sizes, giving birth to very small and underdeveloped young. This is clearly an adaptation to the physiological solutions they have evolved to their period of winter starvation.

There is a problem with this theory, however, in that tropical species of bear do not enter a period of dormancy and the duration for which they do without food is limited to the time when they are nursing their newborn cubs, a period usually lasting only a couple of weeks. Why, then, do these species still give birth to very small, altricial cubs? The most likely explanation is that this reproductive strategy evolved early in the history of modern bears, during the period of glaciation in the northern hemisphere. Under these circumstances early bears would have been under constraints of seasonal food shortages similar to those of today's bears of the northern latitudes. Females would then be under strong selective pressure to give birth early and rear their cubs rapidly. The tropical species evidently evolved from temperate species in which this reproductive strategy had already evolved and it has been retained because it is not negatively selected in areas where there is no seasonal food shortage. The giant panda is an anomaly in this respect since it specialized early to an abundant and constant food source; under such conditions it had no need to develop the mechanisms of winter dormancy found in other bears. The apparent uniqueness of this bear is thus the result of its early divergence from the mainstream of ursine evolution.

Polar bears, also, present something of an anomaly in that they may suffer a period of food shortage during late summer and early autumn. In areas where the sea ice retreats at this time of year, many polar bears stop feeding. Research on American black bears, focusing on the metabolites urea

Bears emerge from their winter dens considerably smaller than when they entered them and have to spend the next weeks fattening up on energy rich foods. This massive loss of weight does not affect their muscle bulk though; all they have lost is the fat stored at the end of the previous year.

and creatinine (the former the product of protein breakdown, the latter produced during normal muscle activity), showed that, whereas creatinine levels in the blood stay more or less constant all year round, urea concentrations alter with respect to feeding activity, becoming very low during starvation. This means that the physiological state of the bear can be described in terms of the ratio of the levels of urea and creatinine in the blood (the U: C ratio). Torpid American black bears have a U:C ratio of less than 10 and this is generally accepted as the level at which an animal can be said to be torpid. When polar bears on the western Hudson Bay were studied in this respect it was found that they too had ratios of less than 10 during the late summer/early autumn period of food shortage; although they spend considerable hours sleeping at this time, they are not in dens and they are not permanently asleep. Nonetheless, they do appear to be in a state similar to the dormancy of other species and the term 'walking torpor' has been coined.

What is even more interesting is that, in the polar bear, this seems to be related to whether or not the animal is eating and is irrespective of the time of year. If an American black bear were to suffer a period of severe food shortage during summer, it would die since it is only capable of using the remarkable starvation physiology during winter. Polar bears seem to be able to alter their physiology at will, entering the 'walking torpor' at any time when food becomes short and waiting for it to become available again. Individuals which feed from garbage dumps during late summer and early autumn do not alter their physiology as do other individuals of the same population which are not feeding and are waiting for the sea ice to reform.

Reproductive Energetics

Females have to acquire, process and transfer sufficient nutrients to their offspring to permit growth up to the time when they are weaned. Since growth will only be able to take place if the net transfer of energy from the mother to her offspring exceeds the amounts required by the young for mere maintenance purposes, the milk has to be both rich and plentiful. Nonetheless there will still be a time when the female's maximal output will be insufficient to meet the demands of her litter; at this time the young will have to start using alternative sources of food to allow continued growth – this is the start of weaning.

Actual growth rates are available for three species of bear; American black-bear cubs increase in mass at a rate of about 77 g (2⅔oz) per day; a rather similar value of about 78.8 g (2⅔oz) per day has been recorded for giant panda cubs. In these species females are about the same size but it has to be remembered that giant pandas usually raise only one cub, whereas American black-bear litters contain two or three; thus the growth rate of the litter is greater for this species. Polar-bear cubs are recorded as increasing in weight by 120 g (4¼oz) per day. Even though the litter size of this bear is similar to that of the American black bear, the size of the female is much greater and thus, if maternal investment is measured in terms of the growth rate of the litter, and taking female mass into account, then both the American black bear and polar bear have similar growth rates.

This growth rate is intimately dependent on milk composition and yield, but milk is expensive for females to produce and so mothers have to balance the rate of milk production against the growth of their cubs, minimizing depletion of their own stored reserves and wastage, but maximizing the rate of cub growth.

Bear-milk composition varies according to species; the percentage of dry matter ranges from 22 per cent in brown and American black bears to 60 per cent in polar bears. There is also considerable variation within a single species: polar-bear milk has been found to possess only 36 per cent dry matter on occasions, whereas American black bears have been recorded as having up to 51 per cent. This variability almost certainly arises since the composition of the milk changes during the period of lactation. American black-bear milk has been shown to almost double its fat content in the first couple of months after the cubs are born; such increases in the fat content, and thus the energy yield, of the milk appears to be common to members of the order Carnivora as a whole. A similar variability of the gross energy yield is also seen; brown-bear and American black-bear milk yields between 6 and 13kJ/g (41 and 88kcal/oz), the milk of giant pandas and sun bears yields about 7kJ/g (47kcal/oz) and polar-bear milk, the richest, yields some 12–20 kJ/g (81–136kcal/oz). Because of this fluctuation it is generally accepted that mid-lactation values should be used for comparative purposes.

Among members of the Carnivora these mid-lactation values are between 18 and 30 per cent dry matter and 4–8kJ/g (27–54kcal/oz) energy yield. Those of bears are typically higher than this with dry matter contents ranging from 27 per cent (sun bear) to 37 per cent (American black bear). Gross energy yields range from 6.7kJ/g (45kcal/oz) in the sun bear to 11.7kJ/g (79kcal/oz) in the American black bear, brown bears falling between these two values at 9.22kJ/g (62kcal/oz). When the dry matter is looked at in terms of its constituents, bears typically show lower amounts of protein and higher amounts of fat than other members of the order; the carbohydrate levels are similar across the order. There are no reliable estimates of the dry matter contents of giant-panda milk. Secretions taken from London Zoo's Chi-Chi, immediately post mortem, suggest values rather lower than those of other bears: 24.5 per cent fat, 4.5 per cent protein and 0.4 per cent carbohydrate. These are very low values for any carnivore and it is difficult to know how much reliance can be placed on them, considering the age of the animal and the fact that it was dead when the specimens were taken.

Although the milk of bears is generally richer than that of other carnivores, the actual intake by individual cubs is more moderate. A 2.3kg (5lb) American black-bear cub drinks about 168g (6oz) of milk per day much the same as the amount taken by a 1.2kg (2½lb) puppy. The rate of milk ingestion in terms of the cub's size though is only 7 per cent, compared with about 20 per cent for domestic dogs and some 77 per cent in mink (*Mustela vison*) kits. This reflects the different energy values of the milk of different species; at mid-lactation, bear milk is almost twice as energy-dense as that of dogs.

It is possible to estimate total maternal milk yield by multiplying the mean milk intake of one cub per day by the size of the litter. In American black bears this gives a value of about 620g (22oz) of milk produced per day by the female. In terms of the mass of the female herself, this value represents some 0.7 per cent of her body weight, markedly lower than estimates calculated for other carnivores (7 per cent in the striped skunk, 8 per cent in the domestic dog and 12 per cent in the American mink). This is due to the extremely small size of newborn bear cubs (making their intake abilities low) and the limited reserves of the female at the end of the prolonged starvation of hibernation. It is quite possible that, once the female starts foraging again and the cubs increase in size, this value would also increase.

As the young develop, their growth requirements increase and, after some time, there has to be a point at which the female is no longer able to meet their demands, although she is producing milk maximally. Female giant pandas and American black bears are more or less the same size and their cubs are weaned at around the same time after they are born (120 days in the case of the black bear; 180 days in giant pandas). Although it is common for pandas to birth more than one young, it is very unusual for them to attempt to raise more than one; black bears regularly are able to rear three cubs. The weights of the cubs show that the investment is similar in both species: the giant panda rears only a single 15kg (33lb) cub, whereas American black bears rear three 4.5kg (2¾lb) cubs; the metabolic mass of the litters of both species are therefore about equal. The peak energy output by female bears is, however, lower than that of other carnivores, e.g. 0.36MJ/day (86kcal/day) for giant pandas and 0.18MJ/day (43kcal/day) for American black bears, compared with 1.02MJ/day (245kcal/day) for domestic dogs, 0.86MJ/day (206kcal/day) for raccoons and 1.1MJ/day (264kcal/day) for the spotted skunk (all values corrected to take account of female body weights). Again this underlines the problems to females of either prolonged starvation during the winter sleep or the dependence on a poorly-digestible food.

Diseases and Parasites

Very little is known about the various conditions from which wild bears may suffer. The natural longevity of bears may be considerable, with the greatest mortality being among subadult animals. Most such deaths occur during interactions with adult males. Although juveniles may also be killed by adult males, this number is not so significant since their mothers are very defensive of their young and also try to avoid areas inhabited by males. Mortality among subadults ranges between 25 and 30 per cent per annum; cub mortality appears higher, ranging between 16 and 44 per cent but, it is common for this to be restricted to the lower part of this range. In addition to adult males, cubs are also in danger from predators, starvation and general accidents. For all species of bear, hunting (both legal and illegal) is the greatest threat to members of any age class.

Bears are no different from any other animal in that they suffer from a range of diseases and illnesses. Many bears are found to suffer from spinal conditions, including inflammation and fusion of vertebrae; these are particularly common among finds of the extinct cave bears of Europe. Some have suggested that the periods of prolonged cave-dwelling during the cold was responsible for this and it is certainly true that bears kept in confined conditions for a long period of time are at risk of developing such conditions. However, in the case of the cave bears, it may be that animals which died due to these conditions are more regularly found than those which were healthy. Cave environments provide a far better chance of fossilization than do open habitats and, since these bears were known to use caves for dormancy purposes, it is very likely that animals would die in them and healthy animals would die in the open, with considerably less chance of being retrieved today.

Internal and external parasites are common: as many as 60 different types have been recorded for bears. As well as the ubiquitous ticks, lice and fleas, bears are also known to harbour protozoans, tapeworms, roundworms, hookworms and flukes. All of these are typically parasitic (they extract a living from, and at the expense of, another animal and differ from predators in that they endeavour to keep their host alive and functioning for as long as possible) and, as such, undoubtedly have a detrimental effect on the bear. Nonetheless, there is very little known about the pathology associated with these organisms and their effect on the life span of the host.

One important parasite of polar and brown bears is the roundworm *Trichinella*; almost all polar bears and some 75 per cent of brown bears seem to harbour this parasite. The most likely source of it in polar bears is believed to be infected seals, although brown bears are not sufficiently dependent on meat in general, and seals in particular, for this to account for the high incidence in them. Possibly the root of this condition in both species is actually fish, polar bears acquiring it secondarily from fish-eating seals. This worm reproduces in the gut of its host, releasing larvae into the bloodstream. These larvae travel around the host's body until they locate an appropriate site at which to encyst, usually muscle tissue. If enough of these encyst in either the heart muscle or brain, the condition is most likely to be fatal. The *Trichinella* parasite will also infect human beings with equal vigour, leading to prolonged, serious and, if untreated, fatal trichinosis. The only way in which human beings can contract the parasite from bears is by eating raw or poorly cooked bear meat, a practice which is quite common among indigenous peoples of the Arctic.

Chapter 5
Behaviour

Bears are almost always referred to as solitary animals, a description which carries the connotation of individual isolation and poorly developed social behaviour. In that bears do not live in large, cohesive groups in the way that, say, wolves do, and that they form no lasting reproductive pair bonds, these facts certainly pertain. However, no animal can be truly described as totally solitary; each inhabits areas through which other members of its species wander and the maintenance of an appropriate spacing between individuals has to involve considerable interaction, albeit at a rather non-physical level.

Animals also have to come together, at least briefly, in order to mate. Courtship usually involves some variable period of contact between two, and sometimes more, individuals; this close proximity may also persist for some time after copulation. Additionally, the period of time females spend with their offspring may be extensive and, even when this bond is eventually broken and the young move away, they may only move short distances, setting up their range in areas neighbouring that of their mother.

In any event, it is clear that even animals which spend most of their time alone, and which attempt to avoid contact with others of their species, still have a rich and varied social life, within which certain aspects of social interaction may be highly developed.

Nonetheless, in bears we do not see the highly integrated social groups which are common amongst other members of the order Carnivora – lions, wolves and African hunting-dogs, for instance. In precisely the same way that group-living in these animals is adaptive, so too is the more solitary existence of bears.

Amongst mammals as a whole, group-living is found predominantly among members of the Carnivora, Cetacea (whales and dolphins), the various ungulate and proto-ungulate groups (deer, antelope, horses, elephants, etc.) and the Primates. It is generally recognized that three main factors predispose animals to group-living. First among these is the enhanced efficiency of hunting as a group as opposed to individuals alone; among many of the larger carnivores this is probably the major determinant. The second factor, important among prey animals, is group defence which may entail actual physical defence or be achieved merely in terms of the increased vigilance resulting from many pairs of eyes. Finally, the nature of the habitat itself may propel certain animals toward living in tight-knit groups; the manner in which food and/or secure living-sites (dens, nests, etc.) are distributed may, in some cases, allow an individual to monopolize a specific area. On the other hand, the converse may be true and an animal might find it almost impossible to defend an area against interlopers; then that individual might be better served by living as a member of a group in that area.

The generally limited amount of predatory behaviour shown by bears offsets the need for group-hunting; even among polar bears hunting seals, the size of the prey and its distribution has not driven the evolution of group predatory behaviours. A single bear in a hunting-group would almost certainly not gain a great deal from such behaviour; in terms of amounts of food actually eaten, bears almost certainly fare better foraging alone. It is also true that the foods upon which bears depend are distributed in such a manner as to make it unnecessary for a group of individuals to band together and collectively defend it from others. Even under conditions where food becomes locally highly abundant as, for instance, in salmon-spawning rivers, there is such an excess of food available that no individual bear's foraging success is reduced by the presence of many others hunting in the same place.

The generally large size of bears and the absence of any natural predators means they also have little to gain from group defence; indeed for most bears the biggest threat they have to face is from other bears. Clearly, therefore, the forces which drive the evolution of group-living in some animals are not pertinent to bears and, in fact, the opposite is true: group-living could actually pose serious disadvantages to individuals.

COMMUNICATION

Sight, sound and smell are the primary sensory channels used by mammals for communicatory purposes. The additional sense of touch, although important among Primates, is rarely found to be used among the other mammalian groups.

Our knowledge of bear communication is poor principally because relatively few studies have been undertaken. Nonetheless, many observations of both wild and captive animals do allow us to draw a number of inferences about how bears communicate with one another and how certain behaviours are important in this respect.

Different sensory channels are used under different conditions: visual signals usually rely on a certain physical proximity between the individuals involved; vocal and olfactory signals are not necessarily so constrained. Olfactory signals, such as scent marks, are not only persistent over quite long periods of time (a feature not usually true of visual and vocal signals) but may also carry considerable amounts of information about the animal which deposited the mark, such as its identity, age, reproductive status and sex.

Differences in physical features (such as pitch, amplitude, frequency and harmonic structure) may permit a range of information to be carried in vocal signals too. Variation of the structure of the call allows the signal to be transmitted over different distances. The main problems involved in acoustic communications are that they are not long-lasting and that they are subject to interference (from other sounds) and attenuation (alteration and 'drop off' of the sound due to distance, physical barriers, echoes, etc.). In the forest habitats preferred by most species of bear these problems are considerable.

Vocal Communication

The acoustic repertoire of an animal is dependent on the structure of the larynx. Among caniform carnivores the ursid form of the larynx is considered to be similar to the ancestral state (suggesting that little evolutionary modification has taken place since the time of *Cephalogale*), as opposed to the more derived structure found among canids and procyonids, both of which have evolved new anatomies which incorporate features peculiar to, and characteristic of, those families. Despite differences in the vocal repertoire and pitch of calls of the giant panda, its larynx most closely resembles that of the bears than that of any other caniform family.

In addition to the obvious vocal sounds which can be made by animals (barks, howls, etc.) there are three other classes of vocal sound production: respiratory, non-respiratory and instrumental. Respiratory sounds are those produced through the mouth or nose and are associated with inhalation or exhalation; these are not the normal sounds found associated with breathing, but rather those produced by exaggerated or stressed ventilation. Such vocalizations have been found to possess specific patterns and durations and can thus be differentiated from the panting sounds which follow exertion. Non-respiratory sounds are those produced in the upper respiratory tract, using the lips, tongue and cheeks; in some animals such sounds may be quite complex. Clearly, there is considerable margin for overlapping use of respiratory and non-respiratory sounds – respiratory sounds produced mainly in the chest may be modified during passage through the mouth, the final sound being a composite of both types.

Instrumental sounds are those produced by banging parts of the body against objects in the environment or against other parts of the body. This would also include sounds produced by objects designed or co-opted for use as instruments; this, however, is a highly specialized form of behaviour and appears to be restricted to ourselves and certain other Primates.

Giant pandas use sound very rarely; particular social activities, most notably courtship, is the commonest incidence. Infant vocalizations have not been well studied but, among adults, a total of 11 different sounds have been recognized as making up their repertoire. Moaning, barking and chirping are all vocal sounds and are used to signify emotional states. Moaning is used as a mild warning whereas chirping seems to indicate higher levels of excitement (especially associated with mating behaviour). Barking appears to be multi-functional and dependent on circumstance; it has been observed to be used when an animal is in a state of alarm or excitement but is also apparently used to give information regarding an individual's position. Huffing, snorting (both non-respiratory) and chomping (instrumental; produced by the teeth and lips as the mouth is snapped closed) sounds are associated with threatening behaviour, the first two being aggressive and the last defensive. Growling and roaring are both unambiguously sounds of offensive threat and possess none of the apprehensive context associated with huffing, snorting and chomping. Honking and squealing sounds (both vocal) denote distress, squealing being used under circumstances of greater anxiety than honking. Both of these sounds appear to act as clear signals, demonstrating lack of aggressive intent. Only a single vocalization – bleating – has been recognized as being used in purely amicable social contexts.

Clearly, giant pandas have a considerable vocal repertoire; varied combinations of these sounds serve to add subtle nuances to their function and some sounds may have different functions depending on the conditions under which they are employed. Considering the dense habitat favoured by these bears, and the limitations this imposes on visual communication,

Although bears are generally fairly quiet, they are able to produce loud roars which they use to communicate their presence and state of mind.

a strong vocal repertoire has obvious adaptive value.

Very little is known about the vocalizations of the small Asian bears, which also preferentially inhabit forested regions. Sloth bears are reported to use nine different vocalizations, one of which is only very rarely heard and possibly acts as a long-distance contact call. The remaining sounds are similar to those used by giant pandas; roaring being used to signify aggressive intent, howling, screaming and squealing all being used during high-intensity threat situations, huffing acting as a warning, and chuffing being used in circumstances of non-aggressive distress. In addition to these sounds sloth-bear cubs have also been heard to use a yelp when distressed – a call which does not appear to be a part of the adult repertoire. Females with young produce a grunting-whickering sound, the function of which has not been fully determined but which may act as an alarm-contact call between the mother and her cubs.

Spectacled bears in South America also inhabit quite densely forested areas. Field studies of this species are not very numerous; most of what is known about their behaviour comes from studies in zoos. Studies of mother-cub vocalization in captive animals suggest that females produce only two sounds: a trill and a growl. The latter is probably threatening whereas the former seems to communicate to the cub that the female is about to change her behaviour in some way. In dense habitats, where a mother and her young may move out of sight of one another, this may be a very useful form of contact vocalization; however, it seems that cubs only respond to this call, in any way, less than 50 per cent of times that it is given. This may mean that the trilling sound has some other purpose, or that it is

Giant pandas have to spend most of their time feeding but they also need to find a mate and males often climb trees to call out to advertise their presence.

redundant in captive conditions where the cub retains visual contact with its mother at all times and therefore has no need to react in any other way than to recognize the call.

The apparent paucity of vocal behaviour among adult female spectacled bears is not necessarily surprising since it is clear that other bears also have restricted vocal communication with their young. Quite possibly, under natural conditions, the range of adult vocal communications may be considerably larger.

Spectacled-bear cubs, on the other hand, have been studied more intensively and they do seem to have a good range of calls; five different sounds have been identified – trill, yelp, whimper, squeal and scream. Cubs usually trill when in physical contact with their mothers and this call may signify contentment, much in the same way that the purring of a cat does. Yelping and whimpering occur most often when cubs are attempting to suckle; whimpering has less urgency about it. Both squealing and screaming are used during conditions of anxiety; subtle variations of these calls occur in different contexts but they are both urgent and of high intensity.

Similar vocalizations are found among other bear species. American black bears tend to be more vocal than brown bears, presumably because they inhabit more forested areas where the effectiveness of visual communication is reduced. Polar bears, which live in the most open habitat of any bear, are the least vocal. The most common vocalization of polar bears is 'chuffing', in which air is expelled in brief, discrete bursts through the open mouth. Similar sounds are made by brown, spectacled and sloth bears. In the latter two species, which live in more enclosed habitats, it is a louder noise and carries further than it does in the case of either the polar or brown bears.

Polar bears employ chuffing vocalizations in a number of different contexts, the function of the call being context-related. Under conditions of high agitation or aggression, a series of chuffing sounds may precede roaring; this type of noise, however, seems to be rarely used by adults under natural conditions. Males use chuffing vocalizations during courtship but by far the commonest circumstance in which this sound is heard is between mother and infant. As with spectacled bears, calling often precedes a change of behaviour by the mother but, again, does not necessarily evoke a response from the infant under captive conditions.

Olfactory Communication

Mammals generally have well-developed senses of smell, the turbinal bones of the nasal cavity being folded and scrolled, thus producing a large surface area for olfactory sensory receptors. Not only are mammals good at picking up scents, some groups are also very effective at producing them. Odiferous compounds may be produced by special glandular areas in various parts of the body and/or be secreted in association with faeces and/or urine. The group which has developed this ability to its highest degree is the Mustelidae – the caniform group of the Carnivora which includes the weasels and stoats, badgers, otters and the undisputed masters of the scent world, the skunks!

Although there is no validated scientific evidence demonstrating that bears use scent marks, several behavioural observations strongly suggest that they do; there are certainly no obvious reasons why they should not!

Behaviours such as rubbing the body against objects (e.g. trees) or along the ground is usually indicative of scent-marking; clawing at trees or the earth may also serve to deposit individual odours. Both brown and American black bears have regularly been observed indulging in such activities and captive brown bears have been seen to urinate on themselves before this rubbing behaviour. Generally, this is confined to adult males and, even then, it is only rarely seen outside of the mating season (although some observations suggest otherwise). Trees marked by clawing and body-rubbing tend to occur along well-used trails in the range and several researchers have suggested that such scent-marking behaviour has a social communication function, most probably serving to maintain inter-individual distance in areas where home ranges overlap (see p.132).

Among the species where such behaviour has been observed, it has been found that (putative) scent marks tend to be deposited in elevated positions; black bears mark trees up to 1.5m (5ft) above the ground; they accomplish this by standing on their hind legs and rubbing themselves against the trunk. Depositing scent marks some distance above ground level increases the efficacy of the mark by ensuring that it is caught by breezes and dispersed over long distances.

Marking behaviour such as this is often accompanied by considerable clawing and biting of the site, often with large amounts of bark being removed. This may serve to announce visually the presence of the marking post; alternatively compounds released from the tree in this way may enhance the odour of the bear's scent.

Bears also seem to be capable of recognizing trails used by other individuals, even in the homogeneous habitat of the Arctic where polar bears have been observed to pick up the trail of other individuals and follow them

Although it is not well documented, it is believed that bears make considerable use of scent marks. This polar bear is sniffing the air, possibly searching for the smell of others of it kind.

Bears may communicate their presence by barking or scratching trees; this may also serve to propagate scent marks which may be deposited during the scratching.

Whereas most bears rub themselves against trees in an upright posture, pandas handstand against trees to deposit scents and during play (as seen here).

for considerable distances in the absence of any visual cues. Such trail-following may be facilitated by the dribbling of urine onto the ground as the animals move around. Alternatively, in habitats where markable objects are present, they most probably rely on such scent posts.

Giant pandas also rub and chew trees but to a lesser extent than other species of bear; these bears also occasionally debark trees in the manner of other bears. They employ urine marks to a considerable extent and have also been observed to use the glandular anogenital area (which is not present in any other species of bear) for marking. The absence of this area in any other bear is correlated, unsurprisingly, with the fact that they are never seen to rub their anal region along the ground or the bases of trees in the way that pandas do. Occasionally giant pandas handstand against trees in order to place their scent at a higher elevation. This is a quite novel piece of behaviour not used by the other species, all of which prefer to stand on their hind legs to reach higher marking posts.

Visual Communication

Compared with many other mammals, bears are fairly uniformly coloured; the giant panda apart, they tend to be only one colour and possess few markings. In those species which do possess them, markings tend to be small and relatively standard from individual to individual. Nonetheless, they may act to exaggerate the size or aspect of an individual during competitive interactions. Certainly, sloth and sun bears rear on their hind legs during such meetings, exposing the markings on their chests; brown bears, however, which do not have such markings, also do this.

The striking facial markings of spectacled bears and giant pandas are almost certainly used to draw attention to the eyes. The dark patches around the eyes of giant pandas are one of the principal reasons for its general popularity, since they give the animal a certain wide-eyed, juvenile appearance which releases protective emotions in us.

Among mammals in general, staring is an aggressive and dominant act producing violent or submissive reactions in the recipient animal. The asocial cats tend to avoid staring and being stared at. Dogs, on the other hand, frequently employ this behaviour in their social groups and violent confrontations may be avoided or precipitated in wolf packs, depending on how secure the challenger feels. You can try this with your pet dog, which

The sun bear has a white spot in the centre of the chest, the function of which is unclear.

The Asiatic black bear, like the sun bear, has a white chest-marking; in this species it takes the form of a chevron extending from the shoulders across the chest.

sees you as the pack leader; almost invariably it will avert its gaze. It is not a good idea to do this continually, however, since the animal will become increasingly insecure and may attack you rather than submitting.

It is very likely that the supra-orbital markings of spectacled bears and giant pandas exaggerate this staring behaviour. Field studies on spectacled bears are few and so it is not possible to determine the natural use of this signal. Giant pandas, however, have often been seen to lower their heads and cover their eyes during non-aggressive interactions or when showing submission.

The rather striking coat pattern of giant pandas has been explained in several ways over time. A popular Chinese story tells of how, upon the death of a young girl who was a special friend of these bears, the pandas at the funeral wept and, on rubbing their eyes with their arms, rubbed the dark colour away from their mourning armbands; in their grief they also hugged themselves and, again, the dark colour of the armbands was deposited on their ears, shoulders, hind legs and rumps.

Two of the more popular scientific theories for this coloration relate to camouflage and heat balance. The camouflage hypothesis suggests that the black and white pattern serves to break up the outline that giant pandas present to other animals. This is similar to the idea given to account for the striped patterns of zebra and tigers; in these two species confusion and camouflage would be very useful and, if it worked, highly adaptive. While it is true that giant pandas merge remarkably well into their snow-covered habitat, it also has to be realized that snow may be present for only 3 months

The dark markings around the eyes of the giant panda are responsible for much of its popularity among human beings.

of the year; in some cases individuals live in almost snow-free areas. This being the case, the white of the coat becomes maladaptively conspicuous and useless in terms of its camouflage potential. It is also true that, today, adult pandas have no natural enemies and thus have little need for protective coloration.

None of this, however, alters the fact that the coat pattern may have originally evolved for camouflage. During the ice ages, pandas may have inhabited areas which were whitened by snow all year round and, in the past, tigers had a much greater range than they do today and would have certainly presented pandas with a strong predation pressure. Evolutionary changes in animals do not happen overnight, especially in cases where there is no disadvantage to their current state. For giant pandas, in the absence of predators, there are no strong driving forces to select for new coat patterns.

Thermoregulation may be important; the ears by virtue of their position and size, would, if white, lose considerable amounts of heat. Being black they are much better insulated and therefore, in cold climates, help to prevent heat loss. The drawback to this particular idea is that it goes no way to explaining the patterning of the rest of the animal.

The true reason for the coat pattern is probably that it offers signals to other individuals. Pandas do not use their face and ears as expressively as do other species of bear, maintaining a rather blank, neutral expression. They also move quite silently through their habitat and it may be that the conspicuous white of their coat serves to alert others to their presence, promoting mutual avoidance and maintaining low levels of contact.

The spectacle-like markings around the eyes of the spectacled bear are quite variable from individual to individual; they may be full circles, which extend down the cheeks, or almost absent.

BEHAVIOUR

Aggressive Behaviour

There can be little doubt that bears are aggressive and dangerous animals; every year infant bears are killed by adult males, large bears maul one another and attacks on human beings occur. The root of this aggressive behaviour (including some human maulings, often the result of a person accidentally wandering into a reproductive situation) is the drive to reproduce.

Biologists recognize today that most aspects of animal behaviour are aimed at the production of as many offspring as possible. Since all reproductively active individuals are employed in the same pursuit, this inevitably leads to conflicts of interest; mostly these are settled by fighting. However, fighting is dangerous to the animals involved and the outcome of physical competition may be that the loser is left permanently maimed or dead, and

The striking coat pattern of the giant panda may serve some camouflage purpose in snow-covered areas. In places where snow is absent the white of the coat becomes maladaptively conspicuous.

The bamboo-forest habitat of the giant panda makes it a very difficult animal to find. The understorey plants are thick and provide easy escape for the bear.

thus unable to meet the biological reproductive directive. For this reason we often find that animals employ alternative competitive strategems, such as impressive displays, bluff, intimidation and large size, to decide the outcome of competitions. Nonetheless, even ritualized combat sometimes breaks down into actual physical fighting, particularly when two more-or-less evenly matched competitors meet. Even then, serious injury may be avoided if one of the combatants breaks off.

Although it is important for individuals to persist in their attempts to achieve the right to reproduce, in the short term, once a conflict has been resolved, the parties involved recognize this and do not generally reinitiate the contest. Over longer periods of time combatants may well meet again; as dominant animals become old and incapable of maintaining their status they will be replaced by younger, more vigorous animals.

Such hierarchical behaviours are known to exist among bears, particularly where large numbers of individuals come together briefly for one reason or another. Salmon-spawning events on Alaskan rivers are one such time when large numbers of brown bears come together for the rich, but ephemeral, food available. The sheer density of this food means that there is plenty for all comers and thus no reason for any individual bear to try to drive others away. In fact, should an individual try to monopolize the resource, it would find itself constantly chasing off other bears and have very little time left for feeding itself. However, certain spots on the rivers are better than others for a variety of reasons – the fish are denser in one place compared to another, or the site is more easily accessible. In such circumstances a bear can dominate one place and easily exclude others from it, but competition to 'own' such a site can be intense.

Under these conditions it is often found that a hierarchy is formed among the bears present, the most dominant individuals fishing at the best sites and subordinates being relegated to more marginal places. Although fighting may be involved in these determinations, size is usually the critical factor, smaller individuals giving way to larger animals without resorting to fighting. Occasionally, a dominant animal may have to remind a subordinate of its status, using growls, teeth-baring and impressive displays of size. Sometimes, when animals fail to take the hint or when a subordinate really feels that it is able to displace the dominant, actual fighting may break out. Extensive scarring and disfigurement is common among older (and some younger) bears and this suggests that the setting up of these hierarchies may involve considerable physical aggression.

Such large-scale aggregations of bears are rare, both within a species and across bears as a whole. The only other species known to form large collections on a regular, annual basis are polar bears. The garbage dumps at Churchill, Canada, are one place where these bears gather every year. Although these are potentially rich food sources, it seems that polar bears would still congregate even if they were not there. The groups tend to be mostly females and young (although there are also males present) and they are waiting for the pack ice to reform so that they can start to move north again. Bears at these dumps show considerably less aggression than do brown bears at salmon rivers since polar bears are not involved in trying to put on weight prior to a period of winter dormancy; competition for food is thus much less intense.

Polar bears are the largest of the bears and, under certain conditions, may become quite competitive. During these interactions they often stand on their hind legs to increase their apparent size.

As a rule the circumstances leading to such aggregations are temporary, with bears rapidly dispersing when the conditions change, returning to their essentially solitary life-styles. However, the urge to mate may also bring individuals into conflict. During the mating season males will be attracted to female scents; this often results in more than one male being attracted to the same female. In such circumstances, physical aggression is almost certainly resorted to; fighting may be intense and individuals may be seriously, or even fatally, wounded.

Since females may spend 2 or 3 years (depending on the species) looking after their young, they cannot become sexually receptive on an annual basis. From the viewpoint of a male, a female with cubs is a lost reproductive opportunity. Clearly, if he were the father of those cubs, this would not be true but there is a good chance that the young were sired by another male, thus compounding the problem since not only is the female currently unavailable for mating but she is rearing the cubs of another male! Under such circumstances there is a strong adaptive value for the male to kill the cubs because this will lead to the female becoming receptive in the next season. It may also help reduce competition between his own cubs and those of another male.

This is a complex scenario in which male and female behaviours are opposed: the female has to rear her cubs, whereas the male has to mate with the female. The solution which bears have adopted to this problem (polygynous, infanticidal males with large, overlapping ranges and defensive, secretive females with smaller ranges and extended periods of parental care) serve to restrict their reproductive success. It may be that the relatively poor lifetime reproductive output of bears is the best that they could hope for, given the restrictions of other aspects of their life history. The mutually exclusive considerations of males and females certainly do not lend themselves to the adoption of a monogamous mating system.

Research has shown that infanticidal behaviour occurs in brown, American black and polar bears, but has not, as yet, been reported in any other species. The foregoing comments defend infanticide as adaptive from the viewpoint of the male. However, the female also has a considerable stake in the cubs and a female which lost her cubs regularly to infanticidal males would have a very poor lifetime reproductive success. For this reason it is not surprising that females put up a spirited defence of their young, often facing up to males which are much larger than they are themselves. Cubs are also adept tree-climbers for the first 6 months of their lives and may escape danger by retreating into a tree. Despite this, 70 per cent of cub mortality is related to attacks by males.

Although some of the early, small species of bear were probably preyed upon heavily by other carnivores, the large size of today's species makes them more or less immune to predation. From time to time wolves or tigers may be able to take bear cubs but the effect of this on the overall mortality of a species is negligible. In areas of North America where both black and brown bears are found one might expect to see some interspecific aggression but the differences between these two species seem to keep this to a minimum. In areas where their ranges overlap, the different types of habitat preferred by the two species serves to keep them separated, the smaller black bears inhabiting forested areas whereas the larger browns prefer the more open spaces.

Although an adult brown bear is able to kill a young black bear, adult brown bears are incompetent tree-climbers and female black bears send their cubs into the trees to escape danger. Young brown bears are less proficient climbers than young black bears and so female brown bears, when confronted by danger, stand their ground and meet the challenge in defence of their cubs.

Spacing Behaviour

The ways in which animals make use of their living-spaces are very variable: some actively defend exclusive territories while others are more tolerant of conspecifics in their home ranges; some animals defend territories all year round while others do so for only specific parts of the year. Two types of living-space are recognized. A territory is an actively defended area from which others of the same species are excluded and may be defended by a group or by lone animals, depending on the level of sociability of the species in question. A home range, on the other hand, is an essentially undefended area and neighbouring home ranges may overlap considerably. Nonetheless, even in home ranges, there is usually an area, known as the core area, which is rigorously defended and which surrounds the den or nest itself. Within these definitions there is considerable gradation, particularly where territories are seasonal.

American black-bear cubs are adept tree-climbers, as are the adults of this species. Tree-climbing is not common among adult brown bears, and black-bear cubs seek protection from this larger species by climbing.

What determines the size and nature of the living-space are the requirements that an animal needs in order to survive. Food, suitable denning-sites and availability of potential mates are all very variable parameters which determine the economic defensibility of an area. For some animals the distribution of some or all of these things may make it inadvisable for a single individual to attempt to exclude all others from the area.

It is generally accepted that bears do not show any typical territorial behaviour. Early reports were equivocal on this matter: some suggested that they were completely non-territorial, maintaining a socially 'neutral' stance; others proposed that they showed a straightforward, typical territoriality. As more and more field research has been conducted, the emerging truth seems to lie somewhere between these two extremes; in certain places, such as at salmon-spawning streams or at whale carcasses, bears may form temporary aggregations where several individuals may be found together with relatively low levels of aggression. However, for many species this is never seen. Indeed, even in those species in which it occurs, there is, for much of the year, little association between individuals and, more importantly, behaviours such as tree-clawing and rubbing, which seem to exist in order to maintain levels of social distance, certainly are seen. On the other hand, no species of bear has been reported to patrol the borders of its living-area regularly, repelling intruders and religiously renewing indications of ownership, such as scent marks; bears are also often found in areas known to be inhabited by other individuals. In a purely logistic sense, we know that the areas over which some bears roam are so large that it would be physically impossible to revisit border marking posts on a sufficiently regular basis to make it worth the animal's while.

The habitat preferences of the different species are quite disparate, ranging from the dense tropical forests of South-East Asia, the home of sun bears, to the vast, open and icy wastes of the north, inhabited by polar bears. Nonetheless, the annual ranging-area of any bear has to be able to meet its survival requirements, namely food and secure denning-sites.

For polar bears, which are the most predatory of all bear species, it is clear that they are constrained to areas in which they are able to find their prey – seals. Due to upwellings of water around coastal margins, which bring planktonic life into the area, large amounts of fish are also attracted to these regions; this in turn attracts seals and they, in their turn, attract bears. The incredibly high productivity of these coastal upwellings are able to support large numbers of seals but these become increasingly rare at higher latitudes. Consequently, although polar bears have been sighted close to the north pole, they tend to be rare there and are found more often on the ice which forms around coastal areas. Such pack ice is not a permanent feature but advances and retreats with the seasons, reaching its most southerly limit during the winter. At this time polar bears may be found in the Labrador, Bering and Barents Seas. On some occasions they have also been found as far south as Iceland and the Japanese island of Hokkaido.

The use of sea ice as a base from which to hunt the seals means that polar bears must alter their range on a seasonal basis with the movements of the ice. In areas where the northern and southern limits of the pack ice change considerably, the annual home range of these bears is vast, in excess of 300,400km^2 (116,000 sq. miles) in some cases. In contrast, individuals

The Arctic habitat of the polar bear provides little in the way of protection. Although polar bears have no natural predators from which they need to hide, they are hunters and thus still need to be able to 'disappear' in their habitat.

living in areas where the annual migrations of the ice is more limited have much smaller annual home ranges, maybe as small as $5,180-7,770\text{km}^2$ (2,000–3,000 sq. miles).

A similar, food-determined variability in home-range size is seen among brown bears. On Kodiak Island, where food is plentiful, the home ranges are much smaller than those of individuals living in mainland coastal regions and these, in turn, are smaller than those of bears living in inland areas.

Superimposed on the nutritionally determined home-range size there are also differences in the sizes of ranges occupied by males and females living in the same area; male brown bears move over ranges some 130–900 per cent greater in area, depending on geographical location, than females. Although males are larger, and thus require more food to maintain their bulk, this cannot be the only reason for the large difference in the sizes of ranges; the degree of sexual size dimorphism is much less than that! In reality the ranges of males have to encompass those of several females so that individual males are more able to maximize their reproductive potential in any one year (see p. 137).

The same is true for the American black bear, where male ranges may be 200–400 per cent the size of those of females. In this species, year-to-year variations in the range area have been documented, which reflect differences in food availability, population density and the reproductive status of the individuals concerned.

On the Ungava Peninsula of northern Quebec (Canada), a population of black bears has colonized a novel and unlikely habitat – the tundra. This area has, due to the hunting activities of Man, lost its population of brown bears. With respect to the average size of American black bears as a whole, these tundra-inhabiting individuals are on the small side and they live by hunting and scavenging. The tundra is generally a poorly productive area, food occurring in patches rather than being evenly dispersed; subsequently the ranges of the bears living in this area are greatly enlarged with respect to home ranges of black bears living in forested areas. Adult males have been found to roam over areas of 55–100km^2 (21–39 sq. miles) and females over 50–200km^2 (19–77 sq. miles). The harsh winter conditions in this area have also led these bears to enter their dens earlier and emerge later than others of their species in less climatically challenging areas: both sexes enter their dens in mid-October to early November; males emerge early next May and females late in May or early in June.

Seasonal variations in habitat quality are less noticeable at lower latitudes where seasonality becomes less and less clear. The bears which occupy such areas (Asiatic black, spectacled and sloth bears) are therefore able to meet their annual survival requirements in a much smaller space. In the Chitwan National Park of India, male sloth bears have ranges of a mere 13km^2 (5 sq. miles) and Asiatic black bears studied at the higher latitudes of northern China roam over areas of some 36.5km^2 (14 sq. miles). In addition, these species are considerably smaller than those found regularly at higher latitudes. Nonetheless, there still exists the discrepancy in the sizes of male and female ranges of individuals living in the same areas.

Although most species demonstrate preferences for one particular type of habitat, the ranges of individuals almost always encompass several types of terrain. Sloth bears, for instance, move from upland areas, which they inhabit over the winter, to lower grassland and riverine forest areas during the summer. American black bears show a strong preference for areas with lots of understorey vegetation but are sufficiently adaptable to inhabit several alternative habitat types, such as the fairly open scrublands of south-western North America and even the swamps of Louisiana.

Such variability of habitat use both by individuals over a season, and within populations, makes it difficult to generalize about habitat preferences and the use of living-spaces. Nevertheless, work on brown bears has elicited three points which can, to a greater or lesser degree, be applied to the other species also. These points all relate to reproductive and nutritional considerations.

Firstly, bears have evolved from the carnivore stock and thus possess guts designed for a diet of flesh. Their secondary move toward a more vegetarian diet has not been accompanied by any gut adaptations to make this less digestible food more easily assimilated; for this reason bears have to rely on the most digestible aspects of the available plant-food spectrum. In order that they be able to locate sufficient quantities of such foods their home ranges have to be extensive. In addition, seasonal variation in the availability of some of their foods has to be taken into account. Some species do not suffer from such constraints. Giant pandas rely heavily on bamboo which is quite well distributed and seasonally constant. Sloth bears, too, as principally termite-eaters, do not suffer from these problems, although lowland areas do become poor in food terms when the wet season arrives and this initiates the shift to higher ground.

The tundra habitat has been colonized by a population of black bears in northern Canada. This type of habitat is quite bleak but does harbour many small rodents which may serve as food.

Female ranges are smaller than those of males, and females with young cubs may have to avoid some of the best food patches in their home ranges in order to avoid the presence of males. The considerable extent of male home ranges seems to allow a single male access to more than one female. The extended period of parental care given by females means that they are not reproductively available every year; in fact a female brown bear will only be receptive once in every 3 years on average. Thus, for a male to make the best of his reproductive potential, his range should encompass those of at least three females.

A final aspect of a bear's home range is that it has to provide suitable denning-sites since bears at higher latitudes spend variable lengths of time during winter in a state of dormancy; at lower latitudes this period is reduced and may even be absent altogether. Nonetheless, even in these cases, dens are important for maternity purposes. Since dens provide security and protection over winter they are very important to the bear and, in some cases, individuals may reuse the same general den area year after year.

Sun, sloth and spectacled bears are not known to enter a period of winter dormancy and, consequently, only the females den while giving birth and for the first few weeks of rearing their young. This is also true of brown bears on Kodiak Island and polar bears in all parts of their range; in both of these cases food is abundant during winter and so nutritional restrictions on activity are relaxed. For the giant panda as well, bamboo food is present

Females of all species of bear enter a den during the winter and it is here that the cubs are born and remain for the first few weeks of life.

all year round. Winter dormancy is therefore correlated with the considerably reduced amounts of food available during this period and is only influenced to a much lesser extent by the inclement climatic conditions which prevail at high latitudes over winter. Such extended winter dormancy is preceded by a period of gorging on abundant autumn foods, generating sufficient reserves to see the animal through the long fast.

The duration of the winter sleep is variable, possibly lasting as long as 7 months for brown bears during severe winters at high latitudes, and as little as 2 weeks in the more southerly areas of the distribution of the American black bear.

Brown bears usually dig their dens in stable hillsides, but may also use brush, snow, log-piles and, on occasion, buildings. American black bears and giant pandas prefer hollow trees, although rock crevices and, in the former, brush-piles and thickets are also used. The maternity dens of polar bears are most often dug out of snow or drifting pack ice. There are three areas which are particularly well known for their high densities of polar-bear maternity dens – the west coast of Hudson Bay, just south of Churchill, Manitoba; Wrangel Island, just off the northeastern Siberian coastline; and Svalbard's Kong Karl Island (Norway).

Courtship and Mating

Courtship behaviours generally serve to acquaint two animals and allow males to gauge the reproductive state of the female. On the whole, bear courtship appears to be a rather brief affair. Females enter oestrus spontaneously. For most species the natural state seems to be a single oestrus period per year, although, in some cases, giant pandas may be able to mate later in the year if they fail to conceive during the spring oestrus; this may also be true of sun bears. In all species the onset of oestrus in females will be accompanied by physiological changes which may, in turn, initiate behavioural changes. In giant pandas oestrogen levels in the blood rise during oestrus, peaking just before the female becomes maximally receptive. Signs of this can be found in the urine as oestrone, a metabolite of oestrogen, the level of which also rises gradually throughout oestrus but which peaks earlier and then falls rapidly. Ovulation in giant pandas seems to be heralded by the presence of the plasma protein *N*-acetyl-ß-D-amino-glucosidase in the urine. Both of these compounds can probably be sensed by males, and females increase their scent-marking behaviour during this period.

Among other species of bear similar changes also occur, although they have not been investigated to the same extent that changes in giant pandas have. Nonetheless, it is possible to see signs of these features in the behaviour of both sexes, females increasing their scent-marking and males regularly sniffing the hindquarters of the females.

Marked behavioural changes may also occur. Female giant pandas become less active as oestrus commences, although they also become very restless; they lose their appetite, the vulva swells and they become more vocal. As female activity reduces, male activity increases; it has also been found that the size of the testes of adult males reaches its greatest during spring, as does the volume of the ejaculate. The male also becomes very vocal during the premating period, in fact more so than the female.

Much of the understanding of courtship and mating in giant pandas is derived from studies of captive animals, of which there have been many, since these bears are notoriously difficult to breed in captivity. Behaviour in the wild seems essentially the same as that observed in captivity, although wild pandas do have the opportunity to engage in some behaviours which the confines of cages do not permit. Considerably more vocal activity occurs in the wild; males often call from trees, their barks and roars carrying for up to 1km (1,100yd). Additionally, since these animals spend much of their time avoiding one another, this shyness is only gradually overcome during the mating season; although the male and female stay fairly close they also remain separate until the female has almost reached her period of peak receptivity. At this time the somewhat restlessly aggressive nature of the female declines and the male which, until this point, has maintained a quite subordinate stance, can move close to the female and initiate copulation.

Despite the lack of information relating to courtship behaviour among other species of bear, available reports suggest a similar picture: males become increasingly aware of females and females become increasingly tolerant of the presence of males until such a time that copulation takes place. American black-bear males visit females repeatedly over a period of 2–3 weeks, assessing the state of readiness of their potential mate. In sun bears this period is equally brief with males visiting females for between 2 and 7 days before copulating. In sloth, Asiatic black and sun bears courtship is reported to involve a lot of boisterous wrestling, hugging and mock fighting, accompanied by barking and clucking vocalizations.

Courting behaviour is important in most mammals. In these Asiatic brown bears (and in other bears also) it helps overcome the more solitary tendencies fostered over the rest of the year.

Polar and brown bears often find themselves in large congregations during the mating season, e.g. where they aggregate around rich food patches, such as garbage dumps, and, in the case of polar bears, at good seal-hunting sites. Under these conditions the normal polygynous behaviour gives way to a much more promiscuous mating system where males *and* females may mate repeatedly with several partners.

For polar bears, the presence of large numbers of individuals increases the level of intermale competition since receptive females will usually be in the company of other males. Once this has been satisfactorily concluded and all but one male has been driven away, the successful male escorts the female to a more secluded area where there is less likelihood of inter-ference and mating can take place. A male and female polar bear will spend 7–10 days in close company and mate repeatedly. High levels of intermale competition may also accompany the mating of giant pandas where the calls of a male may attract the attention of other males. However, rather than competing for access to the female, they seem to form a hierarchy among themselves, the most dominant male securing the right of mating with the female first. Although they may mate more than once, the male seems readily to lose interest whereupon more subordinate males are able to mate with the female, in the presence of the dominant males, with impunity.

The repetitive copulation seen in most bear species is a fairly good indicator that they are induced ovulators, i.e. at the appropriate times of year, females become physiologically ready to ovulate but do not actually do so until they are stimulated by copulation, a certain indicator that at least one male is available. In most bears, although the duration of each copulation is relatively short, they make up for this by mating repeatedly over a period of time. Giant pandas are unique among bears in that they do not stay together for extended periods of time and individual males readily relinquish mating rights to their consorts. Such behaviour is inconsistent with induced ovulation and it is now known that they are spontaneous ovulators, releasing eggs at regular intervals throughout their adult life (a trait which they share with procyonids, such as the red panda).

Eggs are an expensive commodity, not only in terms of the energy and nutrients required to produce them, but also because most mammals have a fixed number of eggs available to them at birth; eggs are released at regular intervals throughout an animal's adult life and, once they have all been used, no more are produced. For this reason it is clear that mammals such as bears, which occupy considerable home ranges and which lead essentially solitary lives, should not 'waste' eggs by releasing them in the absence of reproductively competent males. Ovulation induced through copulation is a strategy which overcomes this problem.

Fitting in with this hypothesis of induced ovulation in bears is the observation that males sequester their mates away from other males and mate repeatedly during this time. For males this period of 'mate-guarding' is important; there is little to be gained in fighting for and securing a female only to copulate once, induce ovulation and then leave so that another male can come along and mate with her with greater chances of fertilizing the egg. There is a benefit in this for females also since the intense competition ensures that she is mated by the 'best' male available. The non-spontaneous nature of the ovulation means that this intermale competition may take place over a couple of weeks, thus further ensuring the female's mate being the fittest, since more males will be involved in these competitions.

The precise physiology of induced ovulation is almost certainly complex. However, it is clear that copulation adds the final stimulus for egg release. In many such cases this requires that each copulatory event be prolonged. In some bears this is the case: copulatory bouts in brown bears, for instance, have been timed at 20–30 minutes each; polar bears on the other hand seem to show copulations of much shorter duration, averaging about 10 minutes. This may indicate that the time spent in copulation is less important as the releaser of ovulation than penile stimulation of the cervix. Among mammals which employ induced ovulation there is usually a stiffening rod embedded in the soft tissue of the penis known as the baculum, or *os penis*. Although this is bony it is not a true bone but rather a sesamoid structure; the extra digit on the hand of the giant panda is such a structure, as is the human patella (knee bone). The actual structure of the baculum is species-specific and serves both to prolong copulation and enhance penile stimulation of the female tract.

Sexual Dimorphism

In any competitive event, such as those in which males endeavour to secure sole reproductive access to one or more females, the advantages of large size are obvious. On the other hand there are also occasions where large size is disadvantageous, such as when finding dens (smaller caves and tree-holes are more common than large ones) and in terms of energy efficiency (a large body takes much more maintaining than does a small one). In many mammals, the balance between these costs and benefits of large and small size gives different optima for males and females, resulting in a sexual size dimorphism. Across the animal kingdom as a whole it is usual for females to be larger than males since the energy they invest in egg production is far greater than that which males put into the production of sperm – females have to be larger in order to produce large, well-supplied eggs. However, among mammals, although the production of gametes is still more costly for females, it is usually the male which is the larger sex (there are some exceptions to this rule, such as the baleen whales, e.g. the blue and humpback). The reason for the large male size is the competition which may exist for access to reproductive females. It is axiomatic in modern behavioural ecology that, where several males compete for receptive females and attempt to sequester some proportion of these females away from other males, there will be large males and smaller females. Such polygynous mating behaviour, although widespread, is not universal among mammals. Some species are monogamous (associate with only one member of the opposite sex either for life or for the breeding season) and, in these, we find that there is little or no size difference between males and females.

Among bears there is no doubt that, in at least some species, there is considerable competition between males for females and therefore it would be expected to see a sexual size dimorphism. Although male polar bears may be two or three times the size of females, in other species, such as sun and sloth bears, the size difference is hardly noticeable.

Bears, following the general mammalian trend, are polygynous; males increase their reproductive success for the season by mating with as many females as they are able to find. In order to do this they have to forego any aspect of rearing their offspring; this is done by the female alone. Such polygynous mating behaviour presents some problems for male bears; the foremost of these is that not all females are receptive every year because of the extended period which the cubs spend with their mothers. This means that, on average, a female bear will be available for mating once every 2–3 years. In most species the large size of the males allows them to cover the ranges of more than one female; even so, any individual male will probably only be able to mate with three or four females in any 3-year period. Polar bears have the most extensive ranges of any bear and it is almost impossible for males to cover the ranges of several females. However, at certain times of the year, males can be sure of finding large numbers of females at specific places (see p. 139). In this species the importance of large size and physical competition is underlined by the high incidence of broken teeth and other injuries sported by males. In brown bears, where females are more widely spaced during the mating season, the ability of males to range over large areas is the foremost consideration and, although there is some evidence of physical combat between males, it is far less than that found among polar-bear males. The sexual size dimorphism of brown bears, nonetheless, is still wide.

Sexual size dimorphism reached its greatest extent among the European cave bears and the American short-faced bears of the Pleistocene (see

Chapter 3). As it is now widely accepted that European cave bears were primarily vegetarian, while the American short-faced bears were strong predators, the presence of this extreme sexual size dimorphism suggests life-styles for these two extinct species which were similar to those of today's brown and polar bears, which lead respectively similar life-styles.

Clearly, sexual size dimorphism would be expected to be greater as the average size of the species gets larger. Thus the largest of the bears (the polar bear) should exhibit the greatest sexual dimorphism, whereas the smallest (the sun bear) should show it to the least degree; this is found to be the case. However, given that all species of bear are essentially polygynous, and that males therefore benefit from greater size, it is interesting to find that the degree of size dimorphism among the smaller species of bear is negligible, much less than can be accounted for by their generally smaller overall size. This is true of American black, sun and sloth bears and giant pandas.

In order to account for this variable degree of sexual dimorphism among bears we have to return to the cost and benefit analysis of size. In each of the species in which we find a less than expected size dimorphism, we also find a preference for habitats in which large size may be a considerable disadvantage. Each of these species spends much of its time in trees and thus the competitive advantages of large size are tempered by its arboreal predilections. Unfortunately, so little is known about the life-styles of some of these bears that it is impossible to comment on their mating system; it may be that males are only able to mate with a single female in any one year since they are unable to effectively cover the ranges of more than two females. Among sun bears, where sexual size dimorphism is almost non-existent, it is even possible that they practise a form of monogamy; reports exist which tell of their travelling in pairs in the wild, occasionally with young. Such reports, however, have not been validated by rigorous study of their mating behaviour.

REPRODUCTIVE PHYSIOLOGY

As with other mammals, following copulation, spermatozoa travel toward the Fallopian tubes where, if ovulation has taken place, the egg is fertilized. After this, the fertilized egg continues toward the uterus and proliferates to the blastocyst stage. Normally the egg then implants into the uterine wall for further development. In bears, however, this is true only up to the point of blastocyst implantation. At this stage, the reproductive physiology enters a period of quiescence which may last several months, depending on the species; this is known as delayed implantation.

For several species of carnivore it has been found that the gestation period is far in excess of that predicted on the basis of the adult body weight (a feature usually closely related to the period of foetal development); in most species this prolongation of gestation is, at least partly, due to an arrest in embryonic development. Such a pause is seen in a number of members of the Carnivora, including mustelids, phocids, otariids and the walrus, and also in the red panda – the only member of the Procyonidae to show this (although in this species it is thought to be variable, the actual period depending on the individual's geographic range). Although it has been suggested to occur in all species of bear, unimplanted blastocysts have only been demonstrated in brown, American black, Asiatic black and sloth bears. The prolonged gestation periods of the other species, however, strongly suggest that it also occurs in them.

The precise physiological mechanism of delayed implantation is unclear; the lack of detailed study of this phenomenon in bears also means that there is no data from which conclusions can be drawn. There have, however, been a number of studies of mustelids and, from these, a basic physiological schema has been identified. The key to the reinitiation of the implantation seems to be changing day length; the altering photoperiod as perceived through the eyes, causes changes in hypothalamic and pituitary functions. Altered pituitary function stimulates increased ovarian activity, specifically of the corpus luteum, which secretes increased levels of progesterone as well as some other proteinaceous factor; together, these secretions induce renewed embryonic development and implantation of the blastocyst. This is most likely achieved by making the uterine environment more conducive to implantation. The failure of implantation to proceed after the initial formation of the blastocyst is due to the absence of these endocrine functions during inconducive day-length conditions.

This picture is not without its problems though; the protein factor secreted by the corpus luteum has yet to be identified and, more importantly, it remains unclear how photoperiod affects pituitary function. This second point is not easily resolved since, in different species, different conditions seem to be important. In stoats (*Mustela erminea*) mating takes place in summer but implantation is delayed until the next spring; presumably the trigger here is increasing day length; European badgers (*Meles meles*) on the other hand seem to reinitiate their embryonic development whilst they are semi-torpid at the end of the year, and so decreasing day length would appear to be the cue. This latter case would also seem to be true of bears where the information, albeit scant, suggests that implantation takes place at the end of the year with birth occurring in the winter den.

Polar, brown, American black and Asiatic black bears are all very similar in terms of the timing of their reproductive behaviours. Polar bear start somewhat earlier, mating taking place between March and June, whereas in the other species it starts in June and lasts through to July. Similarly, births of polar bears are slightly earlier (November to January) than in other species (January to February). Giant pandas mate between March and May, giving birth during August or September; spectacled bears mate later in the year (between May and August) and give birth between January and March. The remaining two species, the sun and sloth bears, are very variable; available information suggests that they may mate and give birth at any time of year. Field studies of sloth bears in India found that mating takes place mostly in June, whereas studies in Sri Lanka found that they may mate over a greater part of the year. A captive sun bear at Berlin Zoo was reported to have given birth twice in 1961: first in April and then again in August.

The total period of gestation is quite similar for most bears – all species except the sun bear and giant panda fall within the range of 180–270 days, larger species having the longer gestation periods. These two exceptions have rather variable gestation times: for sun bears the range is 95–240 days and for giant pandas it is between 97 and 163 days. The available

Giant pandas, like other bears, commonly give birth to more than one infant. It is, however, rare for them to be able to raise more than one to adulthood.

information suggests that, for sun bears, this reflects the variability in mating time; if mating takes place close to the time when food is going to be optimal then there is no need for an extended period of delay. A similar explanation probably holds for the giant panda also; these bears mate between March and May and give birth between August and September. Since the food of this bear is both abundant and constant, the best time to give birth will be mostly determined by climate; a bear which has mated late may have a very attenuated implantation delay and give birth early in August if conditions are good.

The actual duration of the delay is only known for three species. In giant pandas it is variable (between 45 and 120 days), reinforcing the above argument. The other two species are the brown and American black bears, in which the delay is 150 days; this indicates that true gestation lasts for only 70–84 days, a figure comparable with the upper limit of the range for the giant panda (43–75 days). It is likely that true gestation is similar for all bear species with differences in the total period of gestation being accounted for by variable periods of delay in blastocyst implantation.

Litter sizes tend to be small, with four young being the maximum; most individuals of most species give birth to one or two offspring. Giant pandas are unusual in that it is not uncommon for them to produce three or even four young; it is, however, very rare for more than one to be raised to adulthood. Since species living at higher latitudes give birth while in their period of winter dormancy they have the added problem of having to feed their young while not feeding themselves. This is possibly the main reason why the period of true gestation is so short (much shorter than would be expected on the basis of adult body size and very short compared to that of other mammals of comparable size). Unsurprisingly, this short gestation means that offspring are born very small and totally helpless.

Animals which find themselves preyed upon by other animals tend to produce young which are able to walk and run very soon after they have been born; this is known as the 'precocial strategy' and occurs in most antelopes. Animals which do not have this worry are able to produce young which can benefit from an extended period of development after parturition (birth). Young cats and dogs, for instance, are dependent on their mother for a quite extended period of time before they achieve independence; this is called the 'altricial strategy' and bears have taken it to its limit, producing the smallest offspring (relative to the mother's weight) of any eutherian mammal.

The neonate : maternal weight ratio is extreme in bears. For a newborn human child this ratio is about 1:15; comparable ratios among newborn bears are: sun bear 1:100, spectacled bear 1:200, American black bear 1:500 and, for the giant panda, a staggering 1:800 – the lowest such ratio of any eutherian mammal.

Mother-Infant Behaviour

All bears are born blind and helpless and most are also usually described as naked. However, in some species, the infant does have some hair. Polar-bear cubs are covered with a thin layer of fur and so are the cubs of both giant pandas and spectacled bears; in the latter it is possible to make out faint white facial markings soon after birth.

As birth approaches female bears neither eat nor drink, the vulva swells and the nipples become evident. This period of fasting may persist after parturition even in species which do not enter a period of dormancy. In other species this fasting before and after birth is enforced by the fact that females give birth in the seclusion of their maternity dens. In all species for which information exists, birth takes place in a sitting position, the female resting her back against a tree or other solid object. Once the head of the cub is visible the female may assist its emergence by taking hold of it with her paws or teeth. Once the cub has fully emerged it is assisted into a position where it is able to suckle. However, information suggests that, in some species, suckling does not occur straight away, as it does in many other animals, but is delayed for a period of a few hours. The interbirth interval is not known for most bears although, in giant pandas, subsequent infants appear 20–30 minutes after one another.

In giant pandas, once suckling starts, it occurs up to 14 times a day in bouts lasting 30 minutes or so; in spectacled bears the available data suggests that suckling occurs less frequently. Milk is important to infants in more than a merely nutritional sense since it is also the means by which infants acquire immune responses. Young animals rarely have immune competence and antibodies are passed from the mother to her young, firstly through the placenta and then, after parturition, in the mother's milk. Females, by ingesting the faeces of their young, challenge their own immune systems and generate an appropriate response which is passed to the young animal when it suckles. In all bears studied, females spend a considerable amount of time grooming and cleaning their offspring, paying particular attention to the anal region. This stimulates the young to urinate and defaecate;

Bear cubs suckle for up to 1 year after birth. The milk of the female is very rich in fats and, in the early days after birth, also contains antibodies essential for the health of the young animal.

the females then eat the faeces. In addition to presenting the female's immune system with the antigenic challenges of their infants' pathogens, this behaviour also helps keep the den clean. Females, since they are fasting, do not produce any waste.

In most species of bear the female does not leave her young alone during the first few weeks of life. Once she has started eating again and has to leave the den to defaecate, she takes the infant with her. In captive spectacled bears, the female was found to relax her vigilance after just 2 weeks; in both captive and wild giant pandas the period is rather longer. One of the reasons that females need to be in constant contact with their young is to keep them warm; even in those which are born with some hair, it is only a thin covering and of little insulation value. Added to this, is the fact that juvenile animals do not have the nervous co-ordination necessary for shivering and are thus highly dependent on their mothers for warmth.

American black-bear young are born with very weak hind limbs and move around the den by pulling themselves along. Although there is no evidence for this in other species, it is thought likely to occur. Development takes place quite rapidly. In giant pandas the black markings are visible from about day 6 and are all present by day 12 when the coverage of fur is quite dense; the eyes have opened by day 50. In spectacled bears the eyes have opened by day 37 but Asiatic black-bear cubs are reported to have opened their eyes much earlier, by day 10.

Bear milk is very rich; in polar bears it consists of some 30–40 per cent fat. Consequently, by the time the female is ready to leave the maternity den, the infant has grown sufficiently to be able to follow her unassisted;

Bear cubs are very dependent on their mothers for a considerable period of time. In most species the young follow their mothers but in sloth bears the female is often seen carrying the cubs on her back.

this is usually about 2–3 months after birth. Sloth-bear cubs are often seen riding on their mother's backs but, in all other species, the young follow their mothers on foot. Polar bears stay in the area of the maternity den for some 7–10 days after first emerging, cubs sleeping in the den and returning to it during bad weather.

For many species it remains unclear how long the young stay in their mother's company before dispersing. In the giant panda, American black bear and Asiatic black bear, young usually achieve full independence in the second spring, spending just one more winter in their mother's maternity den. However, in some cases this period may be extended, particularly if the female fails to mate during her next oestrus. In the Asiatic black bear and sloth bear it seems that the period for which young may remain with their mother is irrespective of whether or not she successfully mates a second time; there are a number of observations in the wild of females accompanied by infants of two litters.

Sexual maturity occurs after the young disperse; at about 3 years in Asiatic black bears, 4–5 years in American black bears, 5½–6½ years in giant pandas and between 4 and 6 years in brown and polar bears. In these latter two species growth continues after puberty has been reached; male polar and Alaskan brown bears may not achieve their full adult size until they are 11 years old.

Polar-bear cubs spend a long period of time with their mothers before leaving to make their own way; during this period they learn from their mothers how to hunt.

Cub dispersal is usually facilitated by the female abandoning her young rather than the infants moving away under their own volition. Female abandonment is triggered by the increasing drive to find a new mate and the presence of appropriate males. The relatively long duration of the mother-infant association is necessary for the young's protection. Although the major source of cub mortality is adult male bears, other predators may be responsible for some deaths – wolves, tigers and large birds of prey may be able to take small bear cubs. Another important feature of this period is that the mother is able to teach her young about such things as danger, foods, etc. This is particularly important for polar bears, in which species the young have to be competent hunters in order to survive alone. Polar-bear females take their cubs on hunts and allow them to indulge in hunting for themselves.

Play Behaviour

Play is an important behaviour for many mammals in which the young have an extended period of parental supervision. It is unsurprising, therefore, to find that many of the Carnivora have extensive play expression. Although play is most common among juveniles, it is not restricted to them alone; adults also indulge in playful behaviour but usually to a much lesser extent than young animals. Playing does not comprise a unique set of behaviours but mostly involves activities used in other, non-play situations.

Aggressive interactions are not unknown among bears which tend to prefer a solitary life-style. These two sloth bears do not appear to be engaged in a serious fight but rather may be play-fighting.

Play-fighting is important for subadult animals since it assists them in the development of their fighting skills and their ability to judge the strength of other animals without the consequences which often are associated with serious competitions.

Three types of play are recognized: solitary, social with a conspecific, and social with a member of another species. Solitary play usually involves the use of an inanimate object or parts of the animal's own body; it may be expected that this category of play would be the most commonly observed in the predominantly asocial bears. However, this is not the case and play is much more common in social contexts between litter mates, mothers and their offspring, and also among related, and even unrelated, subadults (young animals which are no longer travelling with their mothers). Nonetheless, bears, which are highly dextrous, inquisitive and intelligent animals, do indulge in solitary play; individuals may be seen chasing around for no clear reason and both giant pandas and American black bears have been observed tobogganing down snow-covered slopes.

Social play among conspecifics most often involves play-fighting; running and chasing one another with little or no actual physical contact is less common. Sexual play seems to be very rare and is the behaviour observed least often. Quite detailed observations of juvenile and subadult American black bears, both in captivity and in the wild, have shown that play usually involves sequences of behaviour which are commonly used in other situations but which, during play, are terminated incomplete. For example, play-fighting resembles real fighting in terms of the activities used but never involves erection of the hair around the neck and shoulders, which is almost always seen during real contests. Similarly, play-fighting does not involve the use of many of the vocalizations of real fights and, importantly, lacks the attitudes of threat which convey serious aggressive intent.

Some behaviours are only observed during playful contests: head-butting and muzzle-biting, for instance, are never seen in non-play contexts; head-butting seems to act as an invitation to other animals to play. Under some circumstances, play behaviour may unite sequences of activities which would never be seen used together in non-play situations: prey capture and sexual behaviours, for example, may be seen intermixed during play.

Clearly, in many of these instances, play serves to prepare the young individual for future, more earnest, conflict and for sexual and predatory situations by refining reflexes and allowing animals to 'practise' behaviours without the extreme consequences which may accompany failure during serious interactions. However, play may also serve other functions since it is not solely restricted to cubs. Adult male polar bears have been observed to indulge in playful interactions during which both participants demonstrate mutually predictable and somewhat stereotypic behavioural sequences. Since this is most often observed during the periods of the year when inter-male competitive interactions are absent (e.g. outside of the mating season), it has been suggested that such social play helps individuals to refine their social behaviour and develop their ability to assess competitive opponents in a non-threatening context.

Chapter 6
Conservation

Despite the widespread popularity of bears and their spiritual significance to certain peoples, six of the eight species are today considered to be endangered; only the polar and American black bears are believed to be holding their own – not, however, without some considerable conservation effort, especially on behalf of the polar bear.

Two international bodies are generally referred to in order to determine the status and conservation needs of animals. In the following descriptions, the status of each of the living species is given by reference to the International Union for the Conservation of Nature and Natural Resources (IUCN) and the Convention on International Trade in Endangered Species of Wild Fauna and Flora (CITES) categories.

The IUCN considers the status and 'health' of species and their component geographical populations; species are placed in a category which reflects their current status and their projected future, should no changes be made to the way in which the species or its habitat is treated. The aim of the IUCN is to garner information from scientists and experts internationally and to develop sensible, workable policies for the conservation of both biodiversity and sustainable developments of natural resources. With such information a species may be placed in one of four categories: extinct, endangered, vulnerable or unclassified. 'Extinct' relates to animals for which there have been no sightings in the wild for 50 years (although the species may still exist as captive populations). 'Endangered' indicates that the designated animal is in real danger of becoming extinct and survival is unlikely if recognized causal problems are not dealt with. 'Vulnerable' species are those facing endangered status unless steps are taken to prevent this. 'Unclassified' means either that the species is in no present danger or that there is insufficient knowledge for realistic conclusions to be drawn.

CITES attempts to set guidelines which countries may follow with respect to the trade of their endemic natural resources or species, or with respect to the import or handling of such species from other countries. Appendix I of CITES lists rare and endangered species, the trade in which, for commercial purposes, should not be allowed. This still permits trade for scientific and educational purposes and trade of captive-bred animals. Appendix II lists species which are not currently rare or endangered but which could easily become so if trade is not restricted or regulated.

Despite the international recognition of these two bodies, it is the province of individual countries to police these restrictions. In some cases, financial and manpower resources are inadequate to make this possible; in other cases all that seems to be missing is the desire to comply. A third body, the United States Department of the Interior (USDI) also places certain animals in categories of concern.

The giant panda is one of the rarest mammals in the world; at the last count there were estimated to be no more than 1,100 living in the wild and only 100 more in captivity. It is classified as rare by the IUCN, endangered by the USDI and is on Appendix I of CITES.

Both sun and spectacled bears are also listed on CITES Appendix I. There are estimated to be less than 2,000 spectacled bears in the wild and only 100 in captivity; it is listed as endangered by the IUCN. The sun-bear population is also very much reduced, although there are no reliable estimates of the numbers remaining in the wild. The IUCN also classify this bear as endangered.

The sloth-bear population is thought to be more numerous, with an estimated 7,000–10,000 individuals remaining in the wild. However, due to the recent realization that its numbers are declining, it now appears on Appendix I of CITES and is recognized as endangered by the IUCN. The Asiatic black bear is currently viewed as vulnerable by the IUCN and listed on Appendix I of CITES; the subspecies *Ursus thibetanus gedrosianus*, however, is classified as endangered by both the IUCN and USDI.

There are thought to be approximately 50,000 grizzly bears remaining in western Canada and Alaska, but only 900 in the neighbouring states of the USA (where it is listed as threatened). Of the 100,000 brown bears inhabiting Eurasia, 70,000 are to be found in the former USSR and the surrounding countries alone. The eastern Balkan and northern Scandinavian countries possess a fairly healthy number of brown bears, with a wide, continuous range. However, the populations of western Europe are very much reduced and isolated from one another: Sweden possesses 600 and Finland 400; Norway contains 17 separate populations which have recently been discovered and are thought to be slowly increasing; Czechoslovakia possesses 700 and Yugoslavia 300. In contrast, the Abruzzo National Park of southern Italy contains a mere 70–100 individuals and as few as 8–10 bears reside in the Trentino region of northern Italy. Spain possesses only 80 individuals, most of them in the Carpathian mountains and tragically, it has recently been discovered that there are only about 5 bears left in the French Pyrenees. This desperately low French population is almost certainly on the verge of extinction and could be lost within the next decade. Poland and Austria also contain scant remnants of much larger populations.

All North American subpopulations (excepting *Ursus arctos nelsoni* of Mexico) and all Eurasian populations (except those of the former USSR and surrounding countries) are listed on Appendix II of CITES. *U. a. nelsoni*, *U. a. pruinosus* of Tibet and *U. a. isabellinus* of the mountains of central Asia are all listed on Appendix I. The USDI classify *U. a. nelsoni*, *U. a. pruinosus* and the two Italian populations as endangered; populations in the southern states of the USA are listed as threatened. In contrast, the IUCN consider *U. a. nelsoni* extinct.

The remaining two species, the polar and American black bears, are both listed on Appendix II of CITES. It is not clear how many wild polar bears remain; estimates range from 5,000 to 19,000 and it is classified as vulnerable by the IUCN. The American black bear is considered to sustain the healthiest population of all species of bear. There are estimated to be 400,000–500,000 in the whole of North America; Mexico, however, is now thought to contain only a few hundred individuals. This bear is, as yet, unclassified by the IUCN and USDI, but has recently been placed on Appendix II of CITES in recognition of the fact that its gall bladder is almost indistinguishable from those of sun and Asiatic black bears, making this species a potential new focus for Oriental traditional medicine. The subspecies *Ursus americanus floridanus* of Florida is unofficially considered to be threatened and *U. a. buteolus* is now in imminent danger of extinction. This subspecies formerly ranged from eastern Texas to Mississippi; by the middle of this century its range had been reduced merely to areas bordering the Mississippi and Atchafalanga Rivers of eastern Louisiana.

All of the eight species have, in the past, been found over much larger ranges and at much higher population numbers than exist today. Human activities have been the main, and in some cases possibly the only, cause of the reduction in numbers, through persecution and habitat destruction. As human populations continue to increase, bear populations continue to decline as more and more habitat is claimed for human use. Also, as human populations expand more and more into bear habitat, encounters between the two inevitably increase, usually to the detriment of bears.

CRUELTY TO BEARS, PAST AND PRESENT

Human beings possess a long history of cruelty to bears. The Ancient Romans were particularly barbarous; many kept bears in captivity either as pets or for sport. Both brown and polar bears were used in the arenas: brown bears were forced to fight with dogs and gladiators, and polar bears were pitted against seals in aquatic battles. In a single day in AD 237, a wealthy Roman (later to become Emperor Gordian I) sponsored an event in the Colosseum in which gladiators were said to have killed more than 1,000 bears, exterminating the local populations. Subsequently, emperors sent to northern Europe and North Africa for bears, thus possibly contributing to the eventual extinction of the African subspecies.

The sport of 'bear baiting' had evolved in Europe by the Middle Ages, possibly because the brown bear was just about the only large predator available at that time – lions and tigers, which had previously been used, were unobtainable due to bad trading relations with the rest of the world. This particularly distasteful practice remained popular in Europe for several centuries and continued in many countries well into the eighteenth century; in England it was especially popular (Elizabeth I was an avid supporter) and was not outlawed until the middle of the nineteenth century. The bear used was beaten and blinded and then chained, either by its neck or hind leg, to a stake placed in the centre of the baiting-pit. The animal was then harried by a pack of dogs and men with whips while onlookers cheered them on.

The Americans also possess a cruel history. Throughout most of the nineteenth century Californians arranged prize fights between grizzlies and Spanish bulls; if the bear refused to fight it was goaded into doing so by being provoked with sticks which had nails stuck into the ends of them. This practice was a major factor contributing to the extinction of the Californian grizzly.

Due to their dexterity, agility and intelligence, bears have been trained for performance for hundreds of years; dancing bears have been prominent in

During Roman times bears were forced to fight gladiators in the arenas for the entertainment of the audience. This relief from Miletus, in Turkey, dating from the second century AD, depicts such a contest between a bear and a gladiator.

Indian and Turkish folklore since Ancient times. The practice spread from here into Europe and eventually North America and is still practised today, to a lesser extent, being most prominent in Asia. Despite jurisdiction which now makes it illegal to use wild-caught bears, cubs are still being taken from their mothers, which are invariably killed in the process. Training almost always employs cruel methods, especially as the bears become older. Some reports state that hot plates were placed beneath the bears' feet while music was played; consequently, the animals began to associate music with the hot trays and thus, whenever music was played, the bears would rear up and lift their hind feet in anticipation of pain, so giving the appearance of dancing. Furthermore, in order to assist in leading the bears, a ring, to which a chain is attached, may be inserted through the upper lip, nose or hard palate. Such performing bears were, and are still, forced to work all year round, making it impossible for them to fulfill their natural instinct to enter dormancy. Bears have also been trained to provide amusement as circus entertainment. This was popular as long ago as Roman times and is still occurring today; bears are degraded, being dressed in costumes and forced to perform such tricks as riding bicycles and walking tightropes. In addition to this, they are very often kept in poor conditions and badly cared for.

Bears are no longer pitted against gladiators in arenas and bear-baiting has been illegal for over a century (except in Pakistan). However, cruel so-called sports involving bears still persist. Hounding is very popular and

Persecution of bears has persisted through the ages. Due to persistent hunting, bears became extinct in Britain during the Middle Ages. This tapestry depicts a bear-cub hunt from Devonshire and is dated at about AD 1425–1450.

involves a pack of dogs, fitted with radio-collars, tracking down a bear. The animal is relentlessly pursued, its cubs often being mauled and killed in the process, until the bear climbs a tree to escape – as the dogs raise their heads to look up at the bear, the radio-transmitter signal alters, alerting the hunter on a handheld directional antenna, who is then able to find the bear and shoot it.

Bear-killing in these and similar practices is purely for the amusement of the hunters; many bears, however, are killed for certain items of their anatomy. Rich big-game hunters will pay premium prices to be able to shoot a rare animal and take home a trophy, such as the hide or head. (This type of hunting has been significant in the demise of the brown bear.)

However, a substantial amount of bear persecution has occurred in order to obtain more unusual parts. Bear paws are highly valued, especially in the Orient, where they appear in bear-paw stew and, more commonly, in soup. Restaurants may pay up to US$200 for each paw and up-market restaurants may charge as much as US$850 for a bowl of bear-paw soup. The meat of the left paw is said to be the sweetest since this is the paw believed to be used to take honey from beehives. Apart from the culinary trade, bear paws are also sought by practioners of traditional medicine since they are thought to promote good health. Other parts of a bear's body are also purported to have medicinal properties (a belief carried through from Ancient times) and has consequently led to persecution of the animal. In many countries, bear meat in general is said to be good for rheumatism, weakness and beri-beri; the bones are believed to cure rheumatism and also nervousness in children (as is the blood). The spinal cord is used in the treatment of deafness and giddiness and is also believed to promote hair growth and remove dandruff when rubbed on the scalp. Grease from the back is highly valued as it is believed to promote longevity, strengthen the mind and prevent hunger. In addition, it is used to treat feverish colds, ringworm and baldness, remove pimples and blackheads, and act as a pain-killing lubricant during childbirth.

However, by far the most highly valued bear part is the gall bladder, especially the bile salts it contains. These have been used by traditional Chinese doctors since the sixth century AD and are now used throughout Asia as a medicine which ranks as highly as the rhinoceros horn and wild ginseng. The uses to which practitioners put it vary slightly from country to country; in Japan bear-gall preparations are administered to patients suffering from liver, stomach and intestinal disorders and, in South Korea, it is used to purify the blood and reduce inflammation, a remedy deriving from Ancient Chinese teachings which promote the gall bladder as a 'cold' medicine. Such cold medicines are able to detoxify the body, lower temperature and reduce inflammation. It may also be used to treat eye infections, tooth decay, haemorrhoids, rid the body of certain parasites and alleviate spasms. In some cases it is even used to assist in the curing of such serious illnesses as liver cirrhosis, jaundice, high blood pressure, diabetes, severe burns and heart disease.

The active ingredient in bear bile is ursodeoxycholic acid (UDCA), which only occurs in large quantities in bear gall bladder and has, unfortunately for bears, been scientifically proven to possess medicinal properties. However, UDCA can now be synthesized from cow bile and research is currently underway to determine its effectiveness in various human disorders. Synthetic UDCA is incredibly cheap to produce and could be of great help in stopping the persecution of the world's bears. However, it is still desirable for traditional Asian medical practitioners to obtain it only from bears, in which it is believed to be naturally diluted and buffered to the proper strength and to exist in the most suitable medium for assimilation by the human body.

Many bears are killed for their gall bladder alone and whole carcasses of bears may be left behind to rot. This is because, in comparison, the value of the bear meat is very low; for example, in the mid-1980s, at a public auction in South Korea, a bear gall bladder sold at an equivalent of US$55,000, whereas the meat sold at an equivalent of only US$1,830.

To supply the ever-increasing demand for bear bile, bear farms now exist in China and North and South Korea, in which both black and brown bears are kept in small cramped cages and 'milked' from their gall bladder by a catheter which is permanently implanted in the bile duct. Approximately 10,000 bears are currently held on Chinese bile farms; the Government target is 40,000. Chinese authorities state that this siphoning of the bile is painless and does not affect the bear's growth or breeding ability. Although it may be true that the actual siphoning is painless (and this is debatable), the conditions in which bears are kept certainly inflict considerable stress on the animals and the enforced lifelong immobility causes the limb muscles and bones to atrophy and degenerate. These authorities also claim that these farms are an important step forward in conservation. In contradiction, the main thrust of research in these farms is into increasing birth rates and maximizing bile production; little effort is put into studying the needs of wild bears. Furthermore, by selling bear bile into the general market, these authorities are creating and developing a sustained demand for it; thus hunters still kill wild bears in order to meet this demand. Wild bears are also still being killed since many practitioners believe that farmed bile is inferior to that of wild bears as a result of the lack of exercise in captive animals.

HABITAT REDUCTION

The forms of persecution mentioned in the previous section are a direct threat to bears; however, the most serious threat is an indirect one – habitat destruction. Bears, as large mammals, need lots of space and land clearance has affected, and still is affecting, all bear species all over the world. The human population is increasing at an alarming rate and, consequently, more and more land is needed to support the ever-growing numbers. Thus, natural areas are constantly being destroyed in order to feed, house and provide a living for ever-demanding human beings.

The brown bear once ranged throughout North America, most of Europe and northern Asia and north Africa. Although today it remains the most widely distributed bear species, many of its component populations are small and scattered, large populations remaining only in Alaska, Canada, the former USSR and the Balkan countries.

Large reductions in the numbers of grizzlies on the Great Plains of North America occurred as settlers from Europe arrived in the nineteenth century. As more and more land was taken over to farm livestock, the amount of suitable bear habitat was reduced drastically. Livestock competes with bears by trampling wetland plants and eating spring grasses. In addition to farming, the later development of logging, mining and road-construction industries have caused further intrusions into bear country.

Logging is responsible for the destruction of important foods in the thick underbrush; it also destroys the cover that bears need for rest and safety and, more importantly, may remove specific trees that bears have been using for denning purposes. The whole character of a woodland may be changed after the loggers have finished with it. Research has shown that bears generally do not move away from disturbed areas; this, however, does not mean that bears are not disturbed by the development. The cost to the bear of moving away may be greater than the cost of staying, especially for subadults, since other areas may already be inhabited by other bears. Consequently, a bear living near a developing area may be placed under perpetual stress and not have the option to move elsewhere.

Road construction, as well as changing the habitat, also provides easy access to hunters and poachers, opening up areas previously more or less unreachable.

The combination of hunting, persecution and habitat destruction led to the extinction of the California grizzly by the 1920s. The Mexican grizzly is thought by many also to be extinct and significant populations of grizzlies are now only found in Alaska, the Yukon, the Rocky Mountains of Alberta and British Columbia, and in the mainland Northwest Territories.

Until the late sixteenth century, European brown bears existed as one large population; after this time they began to be significantly affected by increasing human populations, which hunted them for sport and in protection of their livestock. In the last 300 years they have completely disappeared from Germany, Holland and Switzerland and, by the middle of the nineteenth century, all brown bear populations of Europe had been significantly reduced. In Britain they had become extinct by the Middle Ages and, by the middle of the 1940s, there were very few left in the rest of Europe; only a ridiculously small number of havens existed where the bears could live without fear of encountering human beings.

In Japan, brown-bear habitat continues to decline as new farms continue to be built; bears have limited access to rivers (important for food) as the majority are now under human control.

Sloth bears were common in India and Sri Lanka until as recently as 20 years ago; their numbers, however, are now rapidly declining. Although they are not considered game animals, they are hunted for their gall bladders and fat, for use in traditional medicine, and this has had some effect on their numbers. Nonetheless, as with other species, by far the greatest threat to their existence is the destruction of their habitat. The island of Sri Lanka was estimated to have lost 1.85 million ha (46 million acres) of natural high forest between 1956 and 1983. In place of the forest there are farming settlements and hydro-electric power sites. Sloth bears are very shy and are thought to be less adaptable to such disturbance than other species. Another, rather unusual, threat to this bear comes in the form of destruction of termite mounds to provide the fine soil used on tennis courts; termites are an important part of the sloth bears' diet and, without them, there is a high probability that they will starve to death.

The spectacled bears of South America have also been affected. Once abundant in the lowlands as well as the mountains, they are, due to the claiming of land for agriculture, now restricted to isolated forests on mountainsides where human interference is lowest. Sadly, now even these populations are not safe; as farmers exhaust the land below, they are intruding further and further into bear habitat. Some of these cloud forests are in fact protected but many of the farmers possess government permission to use the land. In Venezuela most people do not even know of the spectacled bear's existence, it is so rare. This is because, during the nineteenth century, most wilderness forests between elevations of 700 and 1,700m (2,300 and 5,600ft) were converted into coffee plantations. Then, in the 1940s, a successful malaria eradication campaign was carried out, making previously uninhabitable areas available for human settlement, thus, pushing the spectacled bear further up the mountains; in one area 67.5 per cent of the original forest was lost within a time span of 25 years.

The sun bear still exists in the forests of Bangladesh, Burma, Thailand,

Spectacled bears are becoming rarer and rarer. One of the problems is the destruction of their forest homes in South America to make way for agriculture and human expansion.

Laos, Cambodia, Vietnam, Peninsular Malaysia and the islands of Sumatra and Borneo. It was also, at one time, found in the Yunnan Province of southern China; however, because there have been no recent recorded sightings of the animal in this area, there is some doubt as to its continuing existence here. It is thought to be declining in other areas due to deforestation, which is partitioning the bear habitat into smaller and smaller chunks. One of the dangers associated with forest destruction on such a large scale is the effect it has on the climate – droughts have now become a common feature of Borneo's rainforests.

Although the Asiatic black bear is the species most hunted for its gall bladder, still the biggest threat is destruction of its habitat. Populations are becoming more and more fragmented as human beings encroach further into the mountain valleys which make up its habitat; this has already resulted in small populations of Pakistan, China and Japan becoming extinct.

The range of the giant panda began to decline as long ago as the Late Pleistocene, probably due to climatic changes associated with the glacial advance and the effects of this on vegetation; the later effects of the expansion of human populations compounded this demise. Pandas once ranged throughout the provinces of Henan, Hubei, Hunan, Guizhou and Yunnan; today it is absent from these regions, having disappeared over the past 2,000 years. It now exists in six isolated areas along the eastern rim of the Tibetan Plateau and more than half live in a chain of 13 reserves established by the Chinese Government. Removal of the forest canopy by loggers and farmers has become one of the most serious threats to the panda's existence. This is illustrated by the fact that satellite photos taken over the past 10–15 years have shown the destruction of panda habitat and this has been directly correlated to the decline in panda numbers. The obvious effect of clear-felling (removing all trees) is to destroy the large trees which the pandas need for use as maternity dens, as shelter sites and also for scent-marking. A very serious, but less apparent, effect is the fact that it upsets the natural balance which exists between the trees and bamboo. Bamboo that grows in clear-felled areas is denser, shorter, possibly drier, and possesses more dead leaves in winter than that which grows in natural woodland. Pandas tend to prefer tall culms with wide basal diameters, perhaps because these are easier to select and manipulate than the denser, shorter culms. Selective logging which leaves maturing fir and hemlock standing, providing a cover of at least 30–40 per cent, would be a more preferable method of timber extraction. This would provide denning-sites for the pandas and the shade of these trees would allow the bamboo under-storey to regenerate normally after flowering. However, it is still not known exactly what the long-term effects of this would be on the bamboo.

CONSERVATION GENETICS

Another serious effect of habitat destruction is the way in which it is occurring; certain areas are preferable and also easier to fell. These felled areas, along with roads and railways, as well as natural barriers such as rivers, separate the remaining areas of bear habitat from one another. This leads to habitat fragmentation and results in pockets of isolated individuals. The consequences can be particularly dangerous if the isolated population is made up of only a few animals.

It is now realized that the survival of a species ultimately depends on its overall genetic diversity. A small population will, with time, lose a large proportion of its genetic variation through genetic drift and inbreeding.

Genetic drift is the natural consequence of sexual reproduction and the random mixing of genes which this involves. Natural selection is the process whereby beneficial genes are preserved and deleterious ones are removed from successive generations. However, some genes, which are neither particularly harmful or beneficial, also exist and their effect on an individual's fitness is neutral. The frequency with which such genes are present in a population fluctuates from generation to generation purely by chance. In a population of 1,000 individuals, maybe only 1 per cent, i.e. 10 individuals, carry a copy of a particular gene; in a population of only 10 individuals, this gene will be present in only 0.1 individuals and the chances that this gene will be lost completely from the population are high. The only way such a lost gene can be replaced in a population is by mutation or by the reintroduction of the gene by an animal from a different population. Although this loss may not have an immediate deleterious effect, in the long term it may effect the ability of that population to cope with environmental changes.

Inbreeding has the similar consequence of reducing overall genetic variability, this time through mating with close relatives. Individuals which are closely related to one another are genetically more similar than are unrelated individuals. In order to maximize the incorporation of novel genes into offspring, it is better to mate with unrelated individuals. When populations become small and isolated, this type of outbreeding becomes less and less feasible and inbreeding becomes increasingly likely; since this means mating with genetically very similar individuals it follows that offspring will, over a succession of generations, have markedly reduced genetic variability. Additionally, harmful and potentially lethal genes are exposed through inbreeding.

Both genetic drift and inbreeding result in a reduction of reproductive potential through decreased reproductive rates and small litter sizes. Due to the homogeneity of the gene pool, there is also the risk that the population may be wiped out in one blow, for instance by an epidemic, since no individuals are able to generate any suitable resistance to the pathogen.

It is generally accepted that most species require at least 500 individuals to avoid inbreeding and loss of genes through genetic drift. This is the minimum viable population (MVP); populations which fall below this figure have very little probability of long-term survival. The smallest viable population which will allow short-term survival is calculated to be 50 individuals which are randomly interbreeding. (This figure is not likely to be accurate because random interbreeding only occurs in theory.) As long as several such small populations exist, and as long as it is possible that they may come together for breeding purposes (either naturally or by human intervention), the threat of extinction is reduced. For this reason, if for no other, it is still essential to conserve small populations of bears where they exist.

In many places, small numbers of bears exist in isolation from one another. In 1980, nine of the Chinese panda reserves were estimated to contain less than 50 pandas each, the remaining three containing less than 150 pandas each; in at least one reserve, these had been divided into smaller subpopulations. It is now estimated that pandas exist in approximately 35 isolated populations, most of which contain less than 20 individuals. The spectacled bears of South America have been partitioned in a similar fashion and the brown bear populations of western Europe are all very small and isolated. The French Pyrenean population of 5 individuals is probably the smallest and work is currently underway which aims to reinforce this population. Interestingly, DNA analyses have shown that brown bears from southern Scandinavian countries are genetically more similar to these French bears and it is from here that new individuals will be sought, rather than from the geographically closer, but genetically more distant, Italian populations.

In practice, all bear species, with the possible exception of the polar bear, have been affected to some extent by this population fragmentation. Even the American black bear, which is generally recognized as being the most secure species, has isolated subpopulations which are likely to become extinct if no action is taken to save them.

NATIONAL PARKS

One method of protection for bears comes in the form of national parks – areas designated for conservation purposes but which also encourage visitors; many animals, including bears, rely on these areas for their survival. In 1872 Yellowstone, the first of the American national parks, today famous for its bears, was established. However, even national parks create problems by bringing bears and human beings closer together.

Bears generally seem to prefer to avoid contact with Man and are not, under normal circumstances, particularly aggressive towards human beings. However, sometimes conflict is hard to avoid, especially when the density of people is high; during the months of July and August bear-related injuries are common. In many incidents in North American national parks, bears are provoked and actually exhibit tremendous restraint with the people concerned, often giving a considerable warning before attacking.

Attacks by bears largely occur on hiking trails away from developed areas and at campgrounds where bears are attracted to food. In the past, bears which entered campgrounds were promptly removed, either by transplanting them to remote areas or by shooting them. After 1962 bears were not destroyed until they had become aggressive, caused excessive property damage or injured a camper.

Much time, money and effort has been put into avoiding these confrontations. To prevent injuries occuring on isolated trails, patterns of back-country usage have been changed to minimize the chances of those encounters between human beings and bears which can lead to injury. Trails within areas of dense cover are particularly dangerous and so such hiking routes are being relocated to more open areas. Trails within the home range of a mother with cubs are closed altogether; other paths have been closed during times of heavy bear use. Another way of preventing attacks is by educating the people themselves; hiking parties of six or more seem fairly immune to attack and so large parties are encouraged. If only two people are travelling together, they are advised to make as much noise as possible while hiking through dense cover so that bears will be aware of their presence and be able to avoid them.

Rules regarding storage and carriage of food when hiking or camping in back country also exist. These include burning all rubbish and suspending all food in bags, at least 2.4m (8ft) above ground, from a rope between two trees. Nonetheless, some bears even manage to get at food stored in this manner! Another recommendation is the use of PVC containers, which have proven, so far, to be 'bear proof', and mothballs in a backpack will mask the scent of food.

The highest incidence of conflict, however, occurs around rubbish dumps in campgrounds and also in the grounds of park hotels. This problem has been exacerbated in the past as bears were not discouraged; portable tiered seats were set up at official feeding sites and 'bear shows', complete with ranger-commentary, became favourite tourist attractions. Thus, bears became familiar with human beings and began to raid tents and picnic

Although bears are clearly potentially dangerous animals they are also very popular. They are readily attracted to easy food, such as that found at campsites, where people seem oblivious to the threat they may pose.

tables in search of a meal. Some black bears even tackled cars and developed ingenious methods of getting inside; one particularly clever bear discovered that the way to get into a Volkswagen was to jump up and down on the roof until the doors 'popped' open!

One solution to this problem was to close the rubbish dumps, replacing them with incinerators, thus preventing bears being attracted to camping grounds. Yellowstone-Park managers recognized this problem in the 1960s and decided to close the dumps in 1971. The Craighead brothers, pioneers in grizzly research, advised that this should be done slowly in order to allow those bears that had become almost wholly dependent on the dumps as a source of food time to find and adjust to natural sources. This advice was ignored and, as a result of sudden closure of the dumps, many bears starved to death because of their inability to find an alternative food supply; others were shot in their effort to find food outside the park. Research in the mid-1980s shows that the bear population of Yellowstone still has not recovered.

One possible solution to this particular problem is to provide specific feeding-sites for the bears; these 'eco-centres' would be situated in remote areas of back-country, thus, luring bears away from areas used by human beings. The bears would be fed with the deer and elk harvested from within the park.

Another way of preventing bears from entering habited areas for food is by applying a negative stimulus to the bear when it approaches the area. This method, known as 'aversive conditioning', relies on the association of a certain place or object with something unpleasant, such as a loud noise or repellent odour. Particularly effective are rubber bullets; these give the bears a nasty thwack on the rump and, along with red-pepper sprays, have been the most successful deterrent.

Research has shown that it is usually just a few 'problem' bears which are causing the trouble; it may be that the solution is just to remove these bears by translocating them to more remote areas of the park. In 1978, six parks with a high number of bear incidents set up a joint computer programme – BIMS (the Bear Information Management System) – to store data on bear observations, incidents and management actions. Detailed information on bear incidents and captures for relocation is entered into BIMS for each problem bear. One drawback of relocation, however, is that many bears eventually manage to find their way back home again; certain bears have done this so frequently that they have had to be shot. In such cases, the decision is made using the information stored in the BIMS. People have not helped the situation as they persist in encouraging bears to take food from them, sit babies on their back for photos and indulge in other equally ill-advised activities.

The remote areas to which these problem bears may be transferred have, in some cases, been converted into specific 'bear zones', areas in which bears have priority over human beings. Once a bear zone is declared, any person entering it, for any activity, is provided with a set of rules of conduct and suggestions on how to comply with them. In some areas the idea of bear zones has been expanded and bear sanctuaries have been formed; these are areas protected specifically to provide a refuge for bears. About 300,000ha (0.75 million acres) in North Carolina alone have been devoted to such sanctuaries for black bears. Grizzlies have also received protection in this way: in southwestern Alaska three major sanctuaries have been established. The best known of these is the McNeil River Sanctuary, situated some 200 air miles south of Anchorage. At certain times of the year, this reserve contains the highest concentration of wild brown bears; anywhere up to 56 bears have been seen at the falls at one time. This is because the river is on the migration route for salmon heading back to their spawning-grounds upstream. The river forms a natural bottleneck as a series of cascades restricts the movement of the fish, forcing them to school together and splash their way over the rushing shallow water. Due to its uniqueness, 34,400ha (85,000 acres) along the river was designated as a sanctuary in 1976. One reason for the success of this particular sanctuary is that only a limited number of people are allowed in at any one time. It receives only about 200 people each year (selected by lottery) and these are only permitted in groups of no more than ten at a time and for no longer than 4 days. Furthermore, every activity is tightly supervised by resident biologists who act as guides, encouraging visitors to act calmly and predictably. Food and rubbish are carefully managed so as to prevent bears forming

In many of the USA's National Parks it is common to find bear-warning signs which alert hikers and campers to the dangers of close encounters with these animals and give hints on how to avoid them.

an association between people and food. Because the bears have had no reason to fear human beings they have become remarkably tolerant and will stay and feed at the river even when they are being watched; indeed, this is regarded by many people as the best wildlife-viewing opportunity in the world.

Conflicts between bears and human beings in nature reserves are especially difficult to avoid where human settlements actually occur within the parks themselves. In the Abruzzo National Park, the last stronghold of the brown bear in Italy, there exist five villages, organized as communes, which own 95 per cent of the forested area of the park (66 per cent of the total park area). A further 5 per cent of the parkland is owned privately and used for agriculture. Problems arise because the bears occasionally feed on the villagers' crops and livestock; since 1967 the park has overcome this problem by reimbursing farmers and pastoralists for their losses. Originally supported by the WWF (Italian appeal), this indemnity system is now continued by the park. Although there have been rare instances of bears being shot by the villagers, in general the bears are left in peace, many believing the bear to be an important part of the Italian countryside.

The spectacled bear of South America is less fortunate; much of the cloud forest contained within the boundaries of national parks is being taken over by government-supported settler-farmers or 'campesinos', who are destroying the bears' habitat in order to grow their crops or graze their cattle. As well as the natural range being threatened, bears are also persecuted by the farmers with the excuse that they raid crops. However, research, initiated by 'Libearty' of the World Society for the Protection of Animals (WSPA) has shown that damage by bears has been over-estimated; bears have been found to avoid areas inhabited by human beings and, although they may be responsible for some of the damage, most of the destruction is caused by birds and forest rodents. It has even been suggested that farmers are actively hunting bears in the national parks and that maize is being specifically cultivated in order to attract the bears out of the forest. It is thought that the bears are being killed to supply the demand for bear grease and bile (see p. 158). A major problem for the national parks of South America is that they are run on a very low budget and protective activity is conducted at a minimum level.

The Chinese Government tried to solve their problem of people living on panda reserves by moving the people away from the reserves into newly built villages. Wolong Reserve, as well as supporting 145 pandas (1974 census), houses approximately 2,000 people of the Quiang minority, who are felling the forest. Guards in the forest are reluctant to act because their sympathies lie with the people. The Chinese Government has built new housing for these people further down the valley but the villagers are reluctant to move because their land may have been owned by their family for generations; also new farms may take years to establish themselves. The Government has not enforced this translocation as they are sensitive to the fears of minority groups that they could easily be swamped by the numerically superior Han people. In the past the Government had plans to provide villagers with incentives to change their life-style by, for example, increasing the availability of hydro-electric power and subsidizing the insulation of homes; hydro-electricity rather than wood could then be used for heating and cooking. However, the people have proven reluctant to change from their original methods.

A further problem of national parks is the fact that they are isolated from one another by private land; as discussed previously, this process of fragmentation is a problem for bear populations everywhere. It has been known for bears to cross paved roads, move through cattle land, coffee plantations and swim across rivers; however, these areas are usually no more than 1km (1,100yd) wide. National parks, however, may be separated by areas much greater than this. One solution would be to create natural corridors between areas populated by bears; these corridors should carry the same protection for the bears as do the parks and should be sufficiently large to facilitate immigration into a reserve, thereby increasing, or at least maintaining, species' richness and diversity as well as preventing inbreeding. Furthermore, these corridors should serve to enlarge the foraging area of wide-ranging species, provide a mixture of basic habitats and successional stages of plants to species that require a variety of habitats for different activities during their life cycles and, finally, provide alternative refugia after severe disturbances, such as fire. However, although in some areas this may be theoretically possible, it may not actually come about due to political problems in the country.

The McNeil River Sanctuary in Alaska is one of the prime bear-viewing sites of the world. Tourists are strictly regulated and selected by lottery for the thrill of close viewing of brown bears in their natural habitat.

CAPTIVE BREEDING

The breeding of endangered animals in captivity, with the subsequent aim of reintroducing them into their natural habitat once conditions are suitable, is a relatively new science but one which may have significant application. Although the success of this approach is currently limited, it also has to be borne in mind that our understanding of the techniques, problems and logistics of both captive breeding and rehabilitation of captive-bred animals into the wild is growing. Many zoological gardens, following the excellent example of Jersey Zoo, are now turning their attention in this direction.

The first zoos were established 200 years ago, originally as menageries for public entertainment and, in some part, education. For the first 150 years or so, all animals for display were obtained from the wild. It was only during the 1950s and 1960s that the idea of breeding animals in captivity developed. This was due partly to the financial cost of obtaining wild animals and the monetary value of selling captive-bred rare ones and partly to the challenge itself. During the 1970s, however, it came to be realized that captive breeding could be used as a method to save animals from extinction. As well as being able to reintroduce animals back into the wild, it meant that zoos could obtain their animals by this means, as opposed to extracting them from wild stock.

However, the idea is not as effective as it could have been. Firstly, captive breeding is widely regarded as less cost-effective than aiming to conserve a species in the wild. Some people suggest that, if the funds available to the zoo community were instead used to protect habitats, then many more animals, as well as ecosystems, could be saved; the people of some countries generally believe that, as long as a species survives in captivity, its habitat may be destroyed with impunity. Related to this is the fact that having a captive population of animals may lull people into a false sense of security, relieving pressure on governments to preserve wildlife in natural areas.

Secondly, of course, there is the problem of inbreeding. If, like giant pandas, the animal is very rare, then the world's total supply of captive animals is likely to be too small to promote effective and healthy outbreeding. A further problem in the case of the panda has been deciphering the sex of those in captivity: a number of early attempts to breed these bears were doomed to failure, since two animals of the same sex were placed together in order to mate! The process of artificial insemination was developed in the 1970s and has met with varying degrees of success; Beijing Zoo was the most successful. Now most pandas are kept in China and loaned out to zoos in other countries.

Finally though, there is the problem of the zoos themselves. In the past bears were, and in some cases still are, kept in barren, concrete-lined pits, with little resemblance to their natural habitat. In these pits there is often nowhere for an animal to go to avoid the public eye or their cage-mates, with whom it had been ill-advisedly placed. Bears are basically solitary animals and keeping them in such unnatural social groups and in hard, sterile environments places them under chronic stress. This results in high levels of pituitary-adrenal activity which may have inhibitory effects on reproduction, immune responses, growth and digestion. The barren environmental conditions also induce rigid, unvarying behaviour patterns, such as incessant pacing. This has been found to be especially prominent among captive polar bears; consequently many people now discourage zoos from keeping them, although many still do.

Once a zoo has been successful in getting a female bear pregnant, there is often no solitary retreat, similar to a maternity den in the wild, provided. There are many disturbances, such as the sounds of zoo maintenance and the smells of other bears, and, as a consequence, cub survival has generally not been very high. The stereotypic behaviour patterns brought on by the stressful environment also means that the animals are totally unsuitable for reintroductions to the wild. Thus, the object has been defeated.

Research has shown that two inter-related factors are likely to influence the post-release survival of reintroduced animals: the possession of specific survival skills gained from previous experience, and the capacity to learn new and flexible skills in response to a new, dynamic environment. Both of these factors are influenced by the quality of the pre-release environment. Most bears in zoos have been fed on prepared food which requires no foraging effort and so no naturally beneficial skills are acquired.

Recent research has shown that enrichment can not only reduce the levels of stress-related hormones in zoo animals but also ensure the success of reintroduction programmes by providing animals with the opportunity to learn skills necessary for life in the wild, and by optimizing the capacity of animals to learn from, and adapt to, new environments.

Many zoos now lay sand, soil and pebbles on the bottom of the bear's enclosure, as well as providing tree-trunks and rock mounds in an effort to simulate a bear's natural habitat, thus encouraging more natural behaviour. In addition, play items, such as traffic-cones and hose-pipes, have been given to induce the bear's naturally investigative behaviour. Food and food-delivery regimes have also been changed. Some food (fruit, vegetables, meat, raisins and currants) is chopped up and then distributed throughout the enclosure, thus ensuring that the bears actually spend time seaching for the food (foraging) and so do not become lazy. Food is also being made more interesting for bears by delivering it in different ways. For instance, they are often offered entire carcasses of small animals, as well as shell-fish and food enclosed in plastic containers; all of these require the bear to exercise its manipulative skills using paws, claws and teeth. The main feed occurs in the morning; this reduces the stress associated with the anti-cipation of food, but additional, small meals are also given throughout the day, keeping the animals alert.

Despite its drawbacks, captive breeding may be the only way in which some bears, such as the tropical species, can be preserved. It also entails considerable co-operation between different nations; many zoos throughout the world are now joining together to foster joint bear-breeding programmes. A variety of interconnected mechanisms have now been established to co-ordinate captive-breeding activities in different zoos; these include studbooks and the International Species Inventory System (ISIS).

CONFLICTS OUTSIDE NATIONAL PARKS

Interference between bears and human beings is more apparent where high numbers of bears live outside national-park boundaries, as is the case with

American black bears. However, this species is not especially dangerous and the vast majority of damage is to property rather than human beings. The most serious of such damage occurs to trees in the coastal timber districts of northern California, Oregon, Washington and southern British Columbia. These areas have exceptionally high bear populations which, for most of the year, leave the trees alone. However, during the months of May and June (when little other food is available and the bears are very hungry, having just emerged from hibernation), these bears wreak havoc on trees such as the Douglas fir, western hemlock and western red cedar in order to get at the sugary sapwood. The bears get to the cambium (internal growth tissue of the tree) by stripping off the bark; if bark is removed all the way around the tree then the tree dies. Bears only damage some trees in this way but, even if only part of the bark is removed, the tree becomes susceptible to fungal infections. Thus, bears may cause millions of dollars worth of loss to the timber industry.

In the 1940s the problem became apparent and, to combat it, a special spring hunting season was established, subsequently responsible for thousands of bears being killed; it was estimated in the early 1980s that less than 20 per cent of the original population remained. Nonetheless, even this remnant population was able to cause extensive damage and it was not until 1985 that an alternative solution was sought. This was provided, ironically, by one of the hunters hired to destroy the bears and involved feeding the bears with an inexpensive fruit-pulp mixture. This has proven very successful and, in fact, much cheaper than the cost of tracking down and killing the animals. These methods are now being encouraged in other states where similar problems occur.

Another form of property damage, which also occurs mostly in spring, is to livestock, especially sheep; to prevent livestock-owners shooting bears some states compensate for losses. The problem which arises here though is that farmers make a claim even if they only see a bear feeding on a carcass; the animal itself may have died of other causes, quite unrelated to the bears.

The states of Georgia, Florida and North and South Carolina also suffer property damage by bears, not to trees or livestock, but to beehives. These are very attractive to bears due to the fact that, in addition to young bees, they also contain vast quantities of mouthwatering honey; bee-keepers may suffer hundreds of dollars worth of losses. Consequently, in most states, bee-keepers are legally allowed to kill the bears that do the most damage. In Florida this has led, in some years, to more bears being killed by bee-keepers than by hunters during the hunting season. Alternative methods are encouraged by state biologists, including preventive methods, such as placing the beehives on raised platforms. Aversive conditioning is also being used, employing electric shocks or mixing the honey with a substance that makes the bears temporarily unwell, so that they are unwilling to try it again. Both methods have been successful.

Polar bears aggregate in areas along the western shore of Hudson Bay, situated on the Canadian coast. This is not a national park and surrounds many towns; the probability of conflict is therefore rather high. During winter the bears are dispersed over the sea ice. Hudson Bay is a huge body of water, approximately 1,287km wide and 1,609km long (800 miles

In the past, polar bears congregating at the garbage dump at Churchill, Manitoba, have caused problems. This has largely been overcome by the establishment of a polar bear 'jail' where problem bears can be isolated until the sea ice refreezes and they can make their way north.

by 1,000 miles); during the summer, when this ice melts, the bears move inland (males along the coast and females and subadults further inland). However, towards the end of summer, the bears begin to migrate up to the northern coast of Hudson Bay, where the ice starts to refreeze first. Up to 1,000 bears may follow this migration route, eventually forming the largest concentration of polar bears in the world. The problem lies in the fact that Canada's most northern deepwater port of Churchill, housing up to 800 people, lies on this migration route and, by the end of autumn, after 4 months fasting, the polar bears, especially mothers with cubs and the subadults, are very hungry. Consequently, bears that would usually do their best to avoid human beings are attracted into town to feed at the rubbish dumps. It was noticed that the number of polar bears was starting to increase in the 1960s and, by November 1968, 40 bears could be seen at a dump at one time. As the density of bears increased some property damage ensued and, generally, encounters between human beings and bears also increased, especially since people came to feed and provoke the animals; in one case this led to the death of a young boy. This naturally led to the bears being looked upon unfavourably and ways were sought to deal with them; the first move was to close all tips and form a single, main dump site. In 1971 the Federal Provincial Polar Bear Technical Committee allowed the authorities of the state of Manitoba licence to kill or capture up to 50 polar bears in defence of human life or property. However, the International Fund for Animal Welfare (IFAW) interjected and proposed to translocate the bears that were going to be shot. Unfortunately, this process was expensive and unsuccessful since most of the bears managed to find their way back again; some of these bears were subsequently captured and sent to zoos. In 1981 the Manitoba department devised yet a further solution to the problem – they built a 'polar bear jail' which could hold up to 16 individual bears and 4 family groups. Now problem bears are captured and held in 'jail' until the ice freezes over again. The jail is no attraction to the bears as they are not fed while they are being held; bears usually live on their stored fat at this time. This is an expensive procedure but, so far, it has been more or less successful.

Today, the attitude towards the polar bear has changed as the town has become famous for them and is known as the 'polar bear capital of the world'. Every autumn, tourists flock to see the bears, with the help of a 'tundra buggy' (a sort of bus with large, wide tyres to minimize damage to the tundra) from which people can view the bears in safety and the bears can go about their business with no interference from human beings.

CONSERVATION CO-OPERATION

In the same way that international co-operation is necessary for captive-breeding projects to work, this is also necessary for the success of conservation management plans in the wild.

For thousands of years Inuit Indians have hunted polar bears for fur, meat and the honour associated with killing such a magnificent beast. The Inuit alone, however, posed no threat to the overall status of the polar bear since their hunting methods were too primitive (a shaft of wood, tipped with stone or ivory) and allowed many of the bears to escape; indeed, many of hunters themselves were killed in such dangerous encounters. Consequently, the Inuit revered the bear and viewed it with considerable respect and awe.

Such reverence was little shared by the European explorers who started to arrive in the seventeenth century. The Arctic attracted whalers who began to kill the bears as part of their business, since the bears were attracted in large numbers to the carcasses of whales that were killed. The aim of these European traders was to kill as many bears as they could. Polar bears once existed on the Labrador coast, hunting salmon in the rapids, much like brown bears in Alaska. The earliest records of these bears are from the diaries of the English trapper and trader, George Cartwright, who promptly shot six of them on the spot – being unable to kill more because he had run out of ammunition. The whalers, and subsequently the sealers, killed everything that could be sold for profit; polar-bear skins became very popular in Europe during Victorian times as a sign of wealth and thereby increased the demand. Between 1905 and 1909, Dundee whalers alone killed more than 1,000 polar bears on the ice off eastern Greenland, in the

Churchill is now recognized as the polar-bear 'capital' of the world, attracting thousands of tourists every autumn. From the relative safety of the 'tundra buggy', people are able to watch the bears; the wide wheels of the vehicle are designed to minimize damage to the habitat.

Davis Strait and Hudson Bay. Consequently, by 1930, polar-bear numbers had been drastically reduced and were still on the decline. Nonetheless, the extermination did not stop. Sport hunting of these bears began in 1950 with wealthy clients in luxury yachts from Europe and North America shooting, at point-blank range, swimming bears which had been attracted to seal blubber used as bait. It was not long before planes were incorporated into the hunt; two planes chased and harried the bear until it collapsed and the 'sportsmen' then landed and shot at the exhausted animal. Hunters paid large sums in order to hunt in this fashion as, unsurprisingly, a kill could be guaranteed. In the 1950s the annual number of kills was approximately 600; by the late 1960s this figure had risen to 1,500, at which point it was realized that something had to be done.

In 1956, realizing the extent of the problem, the Soviet authorities banned all hunting in the then USSR. (It has been estimated that over 150,000 polar bears were killed or captured in Soviet Eurasia between the beginning of the eighteenth century and that time.) Polar bears in other countries, however, were still unprotected. What was needed was co-operation between the five polar-bear nations (Canada, Denmark [for Greenland], Norway, the USA and USSR). In 1965, the first international meeting on the conservation of polar bears was held in Fairbanks, Alaska. Here it was agreed that the polar bear represented a circumpolar resource and each nation should initiate a research programme on the bears within its jurisdiction. Until these results were published and made available to other countries, it was agreed that efforts should be put into conserving the polar bear, including protection for cubs and females accompanied by cubs throughout the year and that further meetings should be held.

The IUCN agreed to co-ordinate the exchange of research results. In 1967, a group of polar-bear specialists organized themselves into what is now the IUCN Polar Bear Specialist Group of the Survival Services Commission. This group met every two years (between 1968–1972) to discuss the co-ordination of research and the management of polar bears. Their most important achievement was negotiating the objectives and text of the International Agreement on the Conservation of Polar Bears and their Habitat. This agreement was ratified and signed at Oslo, Norway, in 1973 and was remarkable in that never before, or since, had the five Arctic nations co-operated to such an extent on a shared concern.

The agreement prevents the hunting and capture of polar bears, except under the specific conditions of bona fide scientific research, prevention of serious disturbance of the management of other resources, protection of life and property, and by local indigenous peoples exercising their traditional rights (for subsistence purposes). It does not permit the use of aircraft or large motorized vessels and the skins collected should not be made available for commercial sale. Finally, the agreement states that the ecosystems of which polar bears are a part should also be protected.

The indigenous people have in fact set up their own agreement; the Inuvialuit of Canada and the Inupiat of Alaska both harvest polar bears from the same subpopulation – the Alaskans without any restrictive guidelines, meaning that this subpopulation was vulnerable to overharvesting. Negotiating a formal international agreement to prevent this happening would take a decade or more, possibly too long to save the population, so, in 1988, the Indians of the two countries negotiated their own agreement using current scientific information and in the style of an international agreement. This Inuvialuit-Inupiat agreement is not enforceable in any way; its strength lies in the fact that the native hunters drew it up themselves and so it will be a matter of pride to adhere to the guidelines.

Largely as a result of the International Agreement, many critical areas of polar-bear habitat have gained some degree of legal protection and many national parks and nature reserves were established. The Northeast Svalbard Nature Reserve in Norway became a biosphere reserve, thus ensuring complete protection of many denning areas and summer sanctuaries of polar bears; even scientists may enter by permit only.

Since the first international meeting, an incredible amount of research has been carried out on polar bears and our knowledge of their behaviour, reproduction and population dynamics has been greatly increased. This information has been put to good use in helping to form new hunting regulations and protecting polar-bear habitat.

However, although this agreement has largely been a success, it suffers from two fundamental flaws: firstly, it is not legally enforceable and, secondly, there is no infrastructure to oversee compliance. Furthermore, although due to this agreement overhunting no longer threatens the survival of the polar bear, other threats, in the form of environmental pollution and global climatic change, remain serious. Pollutants from factories blow north to the

Arctic; even pollutants banned a decade ago (e.g. organo-chlorides) may still be causing problems if they have become frozen in the ice. Even some spatially distant activities, such as offshore exploration and development of resources, may effect the habitat detrimentally and also interfere with vital components of the food chain.

Ever since the panda was discovered (in the 1870s) it has been considered a rare species, overshadowed by the threat of extinction. As early as 1946, warnings of the potential extinction of this bear started to be voiced and, in 1949, the panda was declared a National Treasure by the new Communist regime. In 1957 the Chinese Government determined to set up forest reserves and, in 1962, the export of skins was banned; the resolution stipulated that 'the giant panda is a rare and precious animal' and declared that forest reserves would be set up for its protection. Still the giant panda continued to decline and many factors combined to contribute to this loss in numbers.

The greatest threat to the panda, as discussed previously, is destruction of its habitat; currently over 1,000 million people inhabitat China and the demand for timber and agriculture is great. Even though China may have banned commercial logging in the reserves, local peasants still cause a great deal of damage.

Linked to the problem of habitat destruction are two factors, the first of which, isolation, causes problems of inbreeding as pandas become trapped on islands of green amidst 'seas of agriculture'. The second problem concerns the staple food of this bear – bamboo, which has its own rather unusual reproductive strategy. At intervals varying from 40 to 120 years, generally depending on the species, bamboo flowers and then dies. In the past this has not been a problem for pandas and may even be regarded as a good thing as it forces them to expand their range and, consequently, increase their outbreeding potential. As such, this periodic die-off acts as a natural antidote to inbreeding. Even now, the problem may not be too great; if the bamboo flowers in patches, other patches nearby will still be available to the bears. Alternatively, if two species of bamboo are present in the area, pandas are able to survive on one species until the other regenerates. This has been shown to be the case in Wolong and centres set up to rescue 'starving' pandas may not be a good thing, especially if the pandas are not released back into the wild once the bamboo has regenerated. However, flowering is a problem when there is only one species in a panda's habitat, a situation which becomes increasingly likely as refugia get smaller and smaller, since if all the bamboo flowers synchronously, the animals face a real threat of starvation.

In the past the panda has had little to fear from poachers as it is not believed to possess any parts useful to Chinese medicine. However, it does get caught in snares set for musk deer, an animal highly valued for its musk. Although the deer have been protected under the CITES agreement since 1980, a loophole exists as trade in musk is not altogether illegal since deer may be kept legally in captivity; this has not proved very successful and, consequently, the deer are still being poached. Furthermore, panda pelts have suddenly become highly valued (despite being coarse and slightly oily), especially in Japan, where they command a price equivalent to about US$176,000.

Due to low numbers and low reproductive potential, a female panda may not produce her first offspring until she is 7 years of age, and even then may only raise young successfully every 3 years. It is calculated that the population can sustain an annual mortality rate of no greater than approximately 8 per cent. This, plus the fact that the panda is a rather awkward, slow-moving creature that has evolved with very few natural predators and thus a poorly developed ability for self defence, conspire against this animal, preventing it from building a healthy population.

Deforestation also exacerbates this problem to some extent, as the roads built to aid logging also give poachers easy access to the interior of the forests and, consequently, more pandas can be reached.

Another relatively new problem for the pandas comes as a result of the economic liberalization initiatives of Deng Xiaoping; China is now becoming more affluent and as result a new tourist industry has been created in western Sichuan. So far, only the Juizhaigou area has been seriously affected as it is taken over by hotels, waste-disposal systems, cars and buses, etc.

The Chinese have to be highly commended for their efforts to save the panda, which they have taken very seriously; they have stopped commercial logging and set up strict anti-poaching laws. In October 1987, the Chinese Supreme Court warned that anyone found guilty of killing a giant panda or smuggling its fur would be charged under criminal code regulations governing offences that damage the economy and be treated as a serious criminal, risking jail sentences of between 10 years and life, and possibly even the death penalty. They have demonstrated that they are serious and, in October 1989, the first executions for trading in skins were carried out.

In 1986, an education campaign was launched in 5,000 villages and forest farms throughout Sichuan. This aimed to teach farmers and villagers about panda protection, discouraged cutting of bamboo and gave advice on how to care for starving pandas. To maintain interest, local authorities in Sichuan allocated special funds which were to be used to reimburse peasants for panda-related loss or damage.

In May 1980, the Chinese Association for Environmental Sciences, the Ministry of Forestry, Academia Sinica and the WWF drew up a plan of action, the main aspect of which was the creation of a research station at Wolong funded by the Ministry of Forestry and the WWF. At this station research would be conducted on the ecology, population biology and food-selection of free-living pandas and the management and breeding of captive animals. Despite considerable problems, both logistical and political, a vast amount of data has accrued from the work of Chinese scientists under the direction of the American scientist, Dr. George Schaller, based at this and other research stations in China. Paradoxically, the amount of information available about this, the rarest and shyest of bears, now rivals that of much commoner species.

The Chinese Government has now established 13 panda reserves, an area totalling 6,227km^2 (2,400 sq. miles) and representing approximately 50 per cent of the total remaining habitat of the species. This has been an expensive programme requiring the cessation of timber operations in three reserves and the resettlement of over 3,000 people from Tangjiahe Reserve. Rescue centres have cost the Chinese government US$6 million and WWF US$3 million and, when the bamboo flowered in Wolong in 1983, rescue operations cost some US$2 million. However, in spite of all efforts, the population continues to decline.

A new panda-management plan was drawn up in 1989, jointly prepared by the WWF and the Chinese Ministry of Forestry, entitled the *National Conservation Management Plan for the Giant Panda and its Habitat*. This plan proposes the establishment of another 14 panda reserves covering an area of 4,217km² (1,625 sq. miles), bringing a total of 75 per cent of the remaining panda habitat under protection; this additional area aims to re-establish or safeguard connecting areas between reserves thus allowing natural migration of pandas. However, some populations are irrevocably isolated and another part of the plan involves translocating and reintroducing pandas to these areas. So far, however, there have been few successful attempts at translocating pandas from one area to another. Often animals have to be released into a different altitudinal range, with a new species of bamboo as the staple food, and so many animals have found adaptation difficult. Additionally, pandas seem to possess a well-developed homing instinct and many have been able to find their way back to their original home. The new plan proposes that carefully regulated releases of juveniles may be more practical than releasing adults of breeding age.

The plan also has proposals on captive breeding. The initial aim is to breed sufficient animals for the captive population to be self-sustaining and, ultimately, to be able to produce surplus animals for controlled releases. Although there have been some successes with both natural and artificial breeding, on the whole the breeding performance has been poor for a number of reasons. Pandas are reluctant anyway to mate in captivity and the captive population is scattered between a large number of zoos, many only having one animal or an incompatible pair. The problem is exacerbated further due to the practice of loaning pandas to zoos around the world. Zoological gardens will pay considerable sums to borrow a giant panda in the not too unlikely expectation that they can recoup the cost at the gates; pandas have long been a certain crowd-puller! Although such money is welcome and needed, the loan of animals means that they are not available for breeding and overcommercialization of the giant panda has become a controversial conservation issue. Thus, the new plan includes a set of guidelines which should help reconcile the movement and use of pandas in the wild, in zoos and in captive-breeding centres. In essence, these guidelines restrict captive breeding to a few, select centres and all animals for use in such programmes are regulated by a committee which keeps detailed records and advises on the optimal mating pairs. In addition, no wild animals can be taken for captive breeding; any panda 'rescued' must be returned to the wild, unless this is really not feasible. Finally, it recommends that, other than animals transported for bona fide captive breeding, the loan of any panda for exhibit should conform to CITES regulations and that animals loaned for exhibition must not be of competent breeding age.

To ensure successful breeding the plan proposes (echoing findings of earlier studies) that the pair are allowed to get to know one another before the start of the breeding season. Artificial insemination should only be used if there are suitable females but no available males.

Females about to give birth should be isolated from other animals, in a place with minimal disturbances; if the cub is rejected by the mother it should be removed and hand-reared.

The plan also has recommendations for reintroductions of captive pandas into the wild, which so far have not been undertaken. Pandas know instinctively how to deal with bamboo; what they need to learn is where to find bamboo in different seasons according to local conditions and this they learn from their mothers. It would therefore make sense to release young adults (old enough to be immune to predators and aggressive resident pandas) with human guides or wild-caught, experienced, adult foster mothers.

The plan finally includes guidelines on farming outside of the nature reserves and stipulates that no new logging units should be built in panda habitat. Additionally, it contains ideas on how the bans against poaching can be strictly enforced.

STUDYING BEARS

It is clear from the above that, when drawing up a conservation plan for an endangered animal, scientific research plays a key role in determining the needs of that animal. Without it, serious mistakes could be made which may, paradoxically, have detrimental effects on the population concerned.

Researching bears has proven a very difficult task for a number of reasons. Like any large carnivore, they are potentially dangerous and so getting close to them is a risky business. However, they are also very wary of people and will shy away when human beings are in the vicinity, making the whole process of finding them very tricky. Fundamental to this is the fact that all species tend to be found in remote areas of the world, where access is a problem. Furthermore, populations tend to be numerically low and distributed over large areas, making the whole programme time-consuming and expensive.

Due to their rarity and the consequent problems of sightings, in the past most of our knowledge of bear biology has been determined indirectly from the signs they leave behind them; scats, diggings and half-eaten carcasses, for example, give an idea of diet, while tracks help to determine the range of particular animals. Although these methods obviously have severe limitations, they have provided a lot of useful information and are still used to a great extent today.

The most critical information though is gained from trapping, anaesthetizing and marking animals. Trapping a bear, however, is not easy and creates risks, both to bears and human beings. The first immobilizing drugs to be developed proved to be potentially lethal and many bears were accidently killed. However, a combination of two drugs, xylazine and ketamine hydrochloride, have now replaced all other agents and are considered safe; although accidents do still occur, they are very rare. Small bears may be caught before being drugged. This is usually achieved by attaching a spring-loaded foot-snare to a tree on a well-used bear trail; alternatively, baited traps have been made from large-diameter culvert pipes. The animal is then drugged using a syringe attached to a short pole. Large bears are usually immobilized from a distance, without first being trapped, either from a helicopter (in open terrain) or from further away on the ground. In this case, a specially modified shotgun is used which fires an anaesthetic-filled dart at the animal, aimed at the shoulder or rump. The dart is tipped

The level of our knowledge of some species of bear is very poor but, in many countries, this is being addressed by increased research into the ecology and behaviour of these animals. Here scientists gather data from a tranquillized animal.

with a hypodermic needle and fitted with a plunger, so that the drug is injected under the bear's skin upon impact.

The drugs take effect after only a few minutes, allowing researchers to start work rapidly. It is essential that the bear's eyes are dabbed with ointment and covered with a cloth to prevent them from drying out or being injured by direct sunlight due to the loss of the blinking response. Body measurements of the bear are then recorded, along with scar patterns, tooth-wear and breakage, reproductive status and overall health. A tiny premolar tooth is removed, which is later used to determine the age of the animal, by counting the cementum/dentine rings which are formed on a more or less annual basis; the bear is not affected in any way by the loss of this tooth. Fat, blood and milk samples may also be taken to provide information regarding the amount of toxic chemicals present and the level of specific hormones. The bear is then marked; a plastic or metal tag will be clipped onto the ear and a number may be tattooed onto the inside upper lip using specialist pliers. This number provides identification for when the bear may be caught again; the same type of information will then be recorded and compared with that obtained on the previous capture. This identification also assists in mark-recapture studies which are used to estimate the size of a population statistically. Giving animals individual marks is important for behavioural studies as it provides insight into the behaviour of individuals as well as information regarding generalized bear behaviour.

For continuous monitoring of a bear's movements, the animal may be fitted with a radio-collar. A transmitter inside the collar gives out a pulsed signal of a specific frequency which allows the animal to be identified and tracked from distances of 8–10km (5–6 miles); the maximum range is 40–48km (25–30 miles) in flat, interference-free terrain (a rare occurence). Bears can be tracked by researchers on the ground and in airplanes and even, more recently, by satellite, allowing bears to be studied by biologists who are thousands of miles away.

Radio-telemetry provides information regarding home ranges, seasonal movements and dispersal patterns. Some bears are fitted with collars containing a 'mortality circuit' which is activated when the bear makes no movement whatsoever over a certain period, indicating the death of the animal.

Scientific studies provide information which is important for many reasons. In terms of conservation, any attempt to construct a management action plan, captive-breeding programme or reintroduction initiative can only hope to be successful if there is sufficient knowledge available to ensure that inadvisable decisions are avoided.

THE FUTURE OF BEARS

Clearly, bears are particularly vulnerable to extinction. Their low reproductive rate means that they recover slowly from population depletion, are particularly sensitive to toxic chemicals and are susceptible to the various environmental impacts of global climatic change.

Habitat loss is critical; as large mammals they require large ranges to support themselves. This is especially a problem in Asia where deforestation is still occurring at an alarming rate and vast expanses of land are being transformed into barren deserts.

One step towards saving bears would be a changing of attitude; we have to *want* to save the bears and, to do that, we have to appreciate their value. Many people in many countries are indifferent to their plight. The only way to change such an attitude is through education; young people should be especially targeted as these are the people who can make a difference in the future.

Even more research needs to be conducted so we can better our understanding of bears' needs. Our knowledge of sun, sloth and spectacled bears is pitifully poor.

It is uncertain at the moment how successful captive-breeding programmes may be; whether they can actually save a species from extinction. One thing that is certain, however, is that maintaining a species in captivity does not make it right for the same species to be allowed to disappear in the wild.

The plight of bears has now become so great that an organization – 'Libearty' (part of the WSPA) – was formed in 1992 specifically to promote the protection and conservation of bears. Its main achievements to date have been the establishment of rescue centres for the dancing bears of Greece and Turkey, the building of a semi-wild sanctuary for the rescued animals in Greece and the construction of an exercise enclosure for bears in Turkey. Libearty organizers in Turkey are also encouraging education programmes and an animal welfare course is soon to be instituted at one of the universities.

The organization is also carrying out work in South America aimed at the protection of the spectacled bear. Orphaned cubs destined to be sold as pets are being adopted by the group and research carried out concerning crop-damage reported that spectacled bears are responsible for only a minimal amount. Thus, using this evidence, the group hopes to prevent the mis-directed persecution by farmers.

There is also an effort by the organization to ban totally the trade in bear gall bladder products and to discourage bear-farming. This is to be accom-panied by an educational campaign explaining why the ban is being sought and what alternatives to bear bile exist.

These magnificent animals, which mean so many things to so many people, which have filled us with awe, respect and fear for hundreds of thousands of years, which have been familiar companions of the wilderness, should not now suffer in the wake of human indifference and greed.

Glossary

We have included this short glossary of terms to make reading the text easier. Rather than having to trawl through the book to locate the meaning of a particular word you may find it in this list.

Auditory bulla Part of the skull which encloses and protects the auditory apparatus of the middle ear.

Baculum Sesamoid structure, found embedded in the soft tissue of the penis of some mammals, which functions as a stiffening rod and helps prolong copulation. Also known as the *os penis.*

Basal metabolic rate (BMR) Resting rate of an animal's metabolism; usually expressed in terms of the amount of heat produced per hour per square metre of surface area.

Canines Conical teeth lying behind the incisors; in the upper jaw these are the most anterior maxillary teeth.

Carnassial teeth Specialized teeth of the placental order Carnivora, consisting of the last upper pre-molar ($P4$) and the first lower molar ($M1$); these possess shearing blades which occlude against one another as the jaw closes. These teeth are diagnostic of this order.

Carnivora Group of placental mammals which includes dogs, cats, hyaenas, mustelids, viverrids, procyonids and bears. All animals in this group have descended from a common evolutionary stem although not all pursue a carnivorous lifestyles.

Carnivorous Describes animals which have a diet consisting principally of meat.

Crepuscular Active at dawn and dusk.

Delayed implantation Where the fertilized egg remains, for some variable period of time, free floating in the uterus before implantation and further development take place.

Digitigrade Mode of walking in which only the ends of the digits are in contact with the ground.

Diurnal Active during the day.

Eocene Epoch of the Tertiary period lasting from 53 to 35 million years ago. During this time the modern orders of mammals arose.

Eutherian Placental mammals.

Herbivorous Describes animals that have a diet consisting principally of vegetation.

Hibernation Period of extended metabolic quiescence in which there are significant reductions in an animal's physiological mechanisms.

Incisors Front teeth in mammalian jaws; in the upper jaw these teeth are premaxilliary.

Induced ovulation Stimulation of ovulation in the female by copulation.

Juvenile Young animal which is still dependent on its mother.

Marsupials Group of mammals which evolved earlier than the placentals. Mostly these have an attenuated period of embryonic development within the female and the remainder of the gestation takes place in a protective pouch.

Metatherian Marsupial mammal.

Miocene Epoch of the Tertiary period lasting from 25 to 5 million years ago. During this time the modern subfamilies of mammal appeared and there was a large-scale spread of grassland and the radiation of grazing mammals.

Molars Back teeth of mammals; these are the teeth which have no precursors in the 'milk' dentition.

Monogamy Mating system in which a single male and female pair; the bond may last for a reproductive season or for life.

Nocturnal Active at night.

Oestrogens Group of steroid hormones – the principal female sex hormones – responsible for the maturation of females and the development and function of the reproductive organs.

Oestrus Period during which female mammals are receptive to mating. Also known as the 'heat'.

Oligocene Epoch of the Tertiary period lasting from 35 to 25 million years ago. During this time many of the modern families of mammals appeared.

Omnivorous Describes animals that have a diet comprising both meat and vegetation.

Paleocene Earliest epoch of the Tertiary period lasting from 65 to 53 million years ago. During this time archaic mammals dominated the planet.

Pheromones Chemicals released by animals into the environment which can be perceived by other members of the species; often these are sex attractants.

Placentals Mammals in which the young is retained for a long gestation period within the female animal. Also known as eutherians.

Plantigrade Mode of walking in which the whole sole or palm of the limb is in contact with the ground.

Pleistocene Epoch of the Quaternary period lasting from 2 to 0.01 million years ago, a time of widespread glaciation in the northern hemisphere.

Pliocene Most recent epoch of the Tertiary period lasting from 5 to 2 million years ago. During this time many of the modern genera of mammals appeared.

Polygamy Mating system in which several members of one sex mate with one member of the other; in cases where one male mates with several females this is called *polygyny* and where one female mates with several males it is called *polyandry*.

Premolars Teeth immediately posterior to the canines in mammals.

Progesterone Steroid hormone which prepares the uterus for the receiving of the fertilized egg and which maintains the pregnancy.

Quaternary period Second period of the Cenozoic era lasting from 2 million years ago until the present time.

Radial sesamoid The 'false thumb' of the giant panda; a sesamoid structure forming in association with the radial bone of the hand.

Sagittal crest Ridge of bone running along the mid-dorsal surface of the skull; muscles attaching the lower jaw usually arise from this crest.

Sesamoid An accessory bone which develops from connective tissue rather than deriving from the embryonic mesenchyme as do true bones.

Spontaneous ovulation Release of eggs from the ovary at regular intervals throughout a female's life, there being no copulatory stimulation to ovulate.

Subadult Young animal which, although not adult, is living independently of its mother.

Tertiary period Geological age lasting from 65 to 2 million years ago. This was the first of the two periods of the Cenozoic era (the age of mammals) and comprises the Paleocene, Eocene, Oligocene, Miocene and Pliocene epochs.

Testosterone Steroid hormone principally responsible for the secondary sexual development of male mammals and the maintenance of sexual activity.

Torpor State of quiescence similar to hibernation but not involving the same metabolic reductions.

Further Reading

A full list of references on the subject of bears is beyond the scope of this book. Here we have listed what we consider to be some of the best and most informative books and papers on the subject.

Barbeau, M. (1945) 'Bear Mother.' *Journal of American Folklore*, 54: 1–12.

Bruemmer, F. (1987) *World of the Polar Bear*. Northword Press Inc., USA.

Catton, C. (1990) *Pandas*. Christopher Helm, London.

Domico, T. (1988) *Bears of the World*. Facts on File, New York.

Ewer, R. F. (1973) *The Carnivores*. Weidenfeld & Nicholson, New York.

Ford, B. (1981) *Black Bear, The Spirit of the Wilderness*. Houghton Mifflin Co., Boston, Mass.

Gittleman, J. F. & Oftedal, O. (1987) 'Comparative growth and lactation energetics in carnivores.' In: Loudon, A. S. I. & Racey, P. A. (eds) *Reproductive Energetics in Mammals. Symposium of the Zoological Society of London*, 57: 41–78. Oxford Scientific Publishers.

Hallowell, I. A. (1926) 'Bear ceremonialism in the northern hemisphere.' *American Anthropologist*, 2: 1–175.

Kurten, B. (1976) *The Cave Bear Story: Life & Death of a Vanished Animal*. Columbia University Press, New York.

Laidler, K. & Laidler, L. (1992) *Pandas: Giants of the Bamboo Forest*. BBC Books, London.

Laurie, A. & Seidensticker, J (1977) 'The behavioural ecology of the sloth bear.' *Journal of Zoology*, 18: 187–204.

Macdonald, D. (1992) *The Velvet Claw: A Natural History of the Carnivores*. BBC Books, London.

Murie, A. (1981) 'The grizzlies of Mount McKinley.' *US National Park Service Monograph Series*, No. 14.

Rockwell, D. (1991) *Giving Voice to Bear: North American Indian Myths, Rituals and Images of the Bear*. Roberts Rinehart, Canada.

Schaller, G. (1993) *The Last Panda*. University of Chicago Press, Chicago.

Schaller, G., Jinchu, H., Wenshi, P. & Jing, Z. (1985) *The Giant Pandas of Wolong*. University of Chicago Press, Chicago.

Stirling, I. (1988) *Polar Bears*. Blandford Press, London.

Stirling, I. (ed.) (1993) *Bears: a Guide to Every Living Species*. Harper Collins, London.

Index

Page numbers in *italic* refer to black and white illustrations. Page numbers in **bold** refer to colour plates. Textual references may appear on the same pages.